SOUL THEOLOGY

BY HENRY H. MITCHELL

Black Belief
Black Preaching: The Recovery of a Powerful Art

Soul Theology

THE HEART OF AMERICAN BLACK CULTURE

Nicholas C. Cooper-Lewter
and
Henry H. Mitchell

Abingdon Press ● Nashville

SOUL THEOLOGY: *The Heart of American Black Culture*
Copyright © 1986 by Nicholas C. Cooper-Lewter and Henry H. Mitchell

This edition published by Abingdon Press 1991
Previously published by Harper & Row under ISBN 0-06-065764-2

Second Printing 1992

This book is printed on recycled acid-free paper.

Library of Congress Cataloging-in-Publication Data

COOPER-LEWTER, NICHOLAS C.
  Soul theology: the heart of American Black culture / Nicholas
C. Cooper-Lewter and Henry H. Mitchell.
    p. cm.
Originally published: San Francisco: Harper & Row, 1986.
Includes bibliographical references and index.

ISBN 0-687-39125-3 (pbk. : alk. paper)

  1. Afro-Americans—Religion. I. Mitchell, Henry H. II. Title.
[BR563.N4C66 1991]
230'.089'96073—dc20   91-24173

MANUFACTURED IN THE UNITED STATES OF AMERICA

To the Ancestors who over the centuries invented and tested what we call SOUL —the "cloud of witnesses" whose spiritual genius was and is our means of survival and our joy.

Contents

Authors' Preface

Belief systems have been a lifelong concern of the collaborators on this volume, independently and then in concert. The system of greatest interest to both of them has been more commonly thought of as a kind of mystique called *Soul*. All cultures have clusters of core convictions about reality, and none can be understood properly apart from the way they traditionally look at the world.

For many, Soul has referred to a variety of other Black-related items: a style of cooking (Soul food), a complicated handshake, a widely popular genre of music, or an identity (Soul sister or brother). Some, if pressed, would define it more specifically as natural rhythm, emotive spontaneity, or a cultural compulsion to compassion (cf. Haley 1972, 636–39).* Still others would define Soul as the sum of all that is typically or uniquely Black. However, most would simply say that it really defies description, and that one who has to ask what it is can never know. Few terms in American English have assumed such a secure place in everyday language without being precisely defined.

The most completely overlooked aspect of Soul is its cultural view of the world—its folk theology. Blacks, stereotypically admired for their excellence in song, dance, and sports, have a well-tested set of internal convictions quite different from the American majority culture and class. For instance, their very ability to relax and move rhythmically comes from feeling at home in their bodies, largely free of Western culture's dualistic notions of flesh and spirit as deeply antagonistic. This same

*Citations in text include only the author's name, date of publication, and page numbers. For complete bibliographic information on works cited, see the Bibliography following the text.

primal acceptance of body and spirit as one is responsible for Blacks' comparatively greater expression of feelings in public. This is augmented by long traditions of freedom to express emotion in worship, with spirit possession (or shouting) prized rather than inhibited. African culture has for centuries understood society as a literally extended family, sharing despite desperate need of their own.

This book is about the belief system of ordinary people in Black America, and the values and/or healing found therein. The purposes here are: (1) to retrieve and preserve the rich, life-giving affirmations of the Black oral tradition, and (2) to clinically validate and offer a pattern of belief and life that heals minds and spirits, helping to prevent pervasive personal and family disintegration. This practical, street-wise Soul culture has been seriously recorded and studied for its value as a spiritual survival resource. It has then been traced in individual case studies to explore how helpful Soul affirmations have been and can be in the healing of persons of all classes and ethnic groups.

There is a sense in which this revelation has been too long in forming. It was first developed as a course in Black Culture and World View at the Fuller Theological Seminary in Pasadena, and then later at the Ecumenical Center for Black Church Studies in Los Angeles. The material discussed in these courses ten years ago generated high excitement about this "new" body of knowledge. Succeeding years added supporting street data, but there never seemed to be any compelling vision of the format the book should take. Then, providentially, Henry Mitchell let his collaborator Nicholas Cooper-Lewter convince him to attend a very intensive national seminar on therapy in Las Vegas.

The affirmations the therapists attending this conference needed and used in healing were seen to have much in common with those encountered in Black worship, preaching, and street culture. Neither clinic nor church had adequately identified them. Without any apparent piety or religiosity, these professionals worked at giving patients a belief base, because their health and wholeness depended on it. Suddenly the vision of the book took on new dimensions. It could be more than an impressionistic ode to Soul, backed only by street talk and church phrases. There could be unlimited cases to document or validate the same points, and it would be possible to draw them from a wide variety of class types. The hypotheses could be tested over a period of several years. All of this helped to clarify a viable format and create an exciting stimulus for writing, while increasing reader interest and usefulness. Thus an idea whose time had come could now be put into print.

One other word needs to be said. There is a large and growing interest in and literature about belief systems. Not only theologians but philosophers and ethicists, educators and sociologists have come to see beliefs as important to their concerns. Sara Little, an authority on belief systems and the design of Christian education, says that belief systems: (1) help persons find meaning and make sense of life; (2) help maintain community, identity, and continuity; (3) give Christian direction to life; and (4) link the individual and the community to ultimate reality and purpose (Little 1983, 18–21). To this impressive array of functions and values, however, must be added the emphasis and focus of this work. Among oppressed people and all others under major stress, belief systems give healing and empowering support to psychic and spiritual survival. The belief system of Black culture has been doing just this task. A literature of equal seriousness about support is needed to preserve it. This book is offered as a beginning effort in that direction.

Nicholas C. Cooper-Lewter
Henry H. Mitchell

Los Angeles, California and
Richmond, Virginia
September 1985

Acknowledgments

Fresh insights may arise, and breakthroughs of sorts may seem at times to come from some single source. But it is probably never so, certainly not in this case. Profound thanks are due to more people than I actually know about, but those I am aware of surely deserve my gratitude here.

First of all, there are the millions of Blacks in Africa and America who developed and tested the world view that I simply inherited from them. All my life I have been blessed by parents, grandparents, and others who felt an obligation to equip the young with a certain wisdom about life. It looked to them at times like common sense, and again like comfort or hope, or even "good religion." An adage like "reaping what you sow" was undoubtedly considered simple common sense. The point is that succeeding generations were not left to shift for themselves in a hostile world. Silver and gold may have been out of their power to give, but such as they had was shared magnificently. I owe them more than I can say, and more than I had any notion until many years after most of them had gone on.

All of this might have gone for naught, however, had not a teacher at the Union Theological Seminary in New York City given his class on symbolism the assignment of reporting on the symbolism in the churches in which we were working. He sought to alert us to the subtleties of culture, and he urged us to be particularly sensitive and aware. Privately after class I asserted to my professor that the Black church had no symbolism whatever, and I asked for another assignment. The teacher looked at me as if I had lost my mind and then politely gave me a mental thrashing I shall never forget. Needless to say, I found he was right, and I have continued the assignment these more than forty years. The teacher to whom I owe so much at this point was Professor Paul Tillich.

Then I owe a great deal to the members of my first classes on culture and beliefs taught at Fuller Theological Seminary in Pasadena and the Ecumenical Center for Black Church Studies in Los Angeles. I am indebted, for instance, to a White female student at Fuller, named Judy Swank, daughter of missionaries to her native Nigeria. She became my most convincing documentation of African and Black American world view. Raised by Nigerian women, she had severe problems relating to the majority culture when she first came to this country. Yet she was quite at home in the Black communities of Los Angeles. It was ironic that mature adult Blacks, staunchly resisting the very idea of the existence of a Black culture and world view, came to regard her experience as beyond doubt. It was as if, to use the very theme of the culture, she had been providentially planted to help launch this needed exercise in awareness.

In the effort to find and document the folk system, generations of seminary students were willing to eavesdrop in the ghetto, noting spontaneous conversations in streets, alleys, pool halls, parking lots, barber and beauty shops, eating places, and even their own homes. They found a wealth of common theological affirmations, mostly overlooked until now. Many of the contexts in which affirmations are quoted in the later chapters come directly out of class reports. I owe the students a great deal, even as I found the awareness they developed to be a most healing influence in their lives.

Of course, as the Preface acknowledges, all of this would never have been brought to a publishable conclusion had not Nicholas Cooper-Lewter entered the picture. As primary writer, I have been dependent on him for most of the clinical insights and case reports. In this effort to interface theology and therapy, my own contribution was largely theological. Yet in the seemingly endless rewriting required, his insights into the principles of practice and the legalities of publication have been impressive. But at the bottom of it all is a much more important debt. Our professional association began with his work of healing in my life. A massive and well-masked depression due to unresolved grief over the death of our son had all but drained me of any urge or ability to write. It was his analysis and therapeutic influence that freed me to go back to work. My debt to this man thirty years my junior is beyond adequate expression.

Finally, I am grateful for the support and encouragement of every school in which I have taught. In addition to the ones above there are: Colgate Rochester Divinity School/Bexley Hall/ Crozer Theological Seminary, all at Rochester; the American Baptist Seminary of the West at Berkeley and in a Los Angeles extension; the School of Theology at Claremont; the University of LaVerne; Los Angeles Southwest College; California State University at Northridge; and now the School of Theology at Virginia Union University in Richmond.

The most significant support and encouragement of all has come from my wife of forty-one years. My schoolmate at Union, with whom I was united in marriage two days after commencement, Ella Pearson Mitchell, has been inexhaustibly upholding and sustaining for the entire time. Her confidence never flagged, even when I was immobilized with a nameless sorrow. In the days before word processors, she would sit motionless for hours, proofreading my texts. Even with the computer, which she managed to provide as a birthday present with the help of many friends, she is an indispensable resource for clarity and flow. My deep gratitude to her knows no bounds.

Yet, as is always true, if this work is not all it should be, I must take full responsibility for the deficiencies. I only hope that even then, the work done will be helpful in opening up new/old vistas and stimulating the completion of the task.

Henry H. Mitchell

1. Belief Systems, Survival, and Theological Method

The 1984 presidential campaign brought religion into public debate in an unprecedented manner. That controversial topic so long under the rug suddenly surfaced, and the country was once again plunged into serious discussions on faith. Many accused politicians of dragging religion into the arena for purely manipulative purposes. That might be true, but it is also true that everybody everywhere does have beliefs. Nobody, in politics or out of it, makes decisions in a religious vacuum. Everybody has a belief system out of which all value judgments flow. Unuttered or expressed, an assumption inescapably involving some sort of faith determines all conscious choices and influences all unthinking response.

The following vignettes from outside organized orthodoxy or church life illustrate the point:

(1) The scene is a large holding cell in the New Orleans city jail, filled at the moment with a cross section of the city's most active pushers, dealers, and addicts. The discussion centers around the question of who might have leaked the evidence that made possible this comprehensive sweep of the local dope trade. Suddenly the conversation switches to a newcomer to the cell, a man who, unlike the others, has been allowed to keep his watch and his belt. All the inmates listen intently as Luke speaks up. He is a leader in the trade, known as "priest of the pimps and rabbi of the violators." In a studied, low monotone Luke says: "They remove your belt to keep you from hanging yourself. . . . They could give me a rope, and I wouldn't hang myself. *God has never put a thing on this earth that he didn't make man strong enough to withstand*" (St. Cyr 1972, 59).

To ward off suspicion, the undercover narcotics agent responsible for the raid had been included among the arrested. He wrote later that he knew now why Luke was so respected. "This philosophical truth would sustain me in the face of adversities for the remainder of my life" (St. Cyr 1972, 58). Luke's testimony was all the more meaningful because he was facing his very first conviction and prison sentence. He already knew he was capable of surviving.

(2) Bob Lucas, a *Jet* magazine reporter, interviews Lola Falana, a star with top billing on the Las Vegas club circuit. The questions center around her extremely strenuous work schedule and the fact she sits at a table unaccompanied. She easily describes her way of handling this difficult load: "Right now I'm drawing on my reserves, and I'm living a very quiet, aloof kind of lifestyle. But I'm not lonely. I'm a strong young woman. When I feel that reserve is running much too low for me to carry my dignity, then I'll do what I must do about it. But I also believe that when that time comes, God will know what my needs are and will supply. *He gives you no more than you can carry*" (Lucas 1979, 25).

Both of these vignettes illustrate the most popular belief or doctrine in the Black worlds of either church or street: the Providence of God. The version quoted in both of these settings recalls a popular gospel song written during the Great Depression. When life was very difficult, Roberta Martin paraphrased the comforting word of the Apostle Paul in 1 Corinthians, "But God is faithful who will not suffer you to be tempted above that ye are able; but will with the temptation also make a way of escape, that ye may be able to bear it" (10:13). Her song, echoed in all sectors of the Black neighborhood, declares; "He knows, yes, he knows, just how much you can bear."

These testimonies will no doubt seem strange to those outside the Black ghetto, who usually view it in negative terms. However, these informal theological statements suggest that people who grow up in the traditional Black community are spontaneously equipped with a system of core beliefs. In the ghetto there is a lot of joking around, great music and dancing, and outstanding athletics, but there is also a lot of deep faith. Why has it remained so strong, and what connection does this core belief have with emotional balance and wholeness?

Let us begin by looking at the phrase *core belief* and how this approach to faith may suggest a whole new way of doing the task of theology.

Core beliefs are much more than easily mouthed shibboleths or conformist creeds. They are the bedrock attitudes that govern all deliberate behavior and relationships and also all spontaneous responses to crises. Panic or calm may be considered functions of human conditioning and personality, but even these responses reflect beliefs that have been learned in some way. Often poorly articulated, if indeed they are expressed at all, core beliefs are our working opinions about whether God can be trusted. Core beliefs are often mistaken for innate characteristics, because they are buried so deep. But they are not inherited or beyond the influences of training and spiritual discipline. They have been acquired through life experiences, worship, and cultural exposure, and they can be altered likewise. Core beliefs are not mere propositions to which assent is given. They are the ways one trusts or fails to trust. They are embraced intuitively and emotionally, with or without the ability to express them rationally. Core beliefs are perhaps most authentically expressed when uttered spontaneously in crisis situations.

Further, core beliefs are distinguished from theological niceties and technical formulations. They contrast sharply with the Greek-influenced elaborations on the Trinity. Spirituals and gospel songs bespeak the deep belief in Jesus Christ common among the sisters and brothers of the Soul community, but their core belief about reality is about one God. Theories about and practices of the presence of the Holy Spirit prevail in the ghetto. But the expressions of faith that issue from the depths of the souls of Blacks do not technically specify facets of the Godhead. True faith or core belief has to do with the response of *all* sectors of consciousness (rational, intuitive, and emotive in concert) to the slings and arrows of outrageous misfortune, and to the life abundant as well. The issue is not the correctness of formulation but the adequacy of trust in the Creator, as evidenced by the ability to cope with one's life experiences. At the point where core beliefs critically operate, the grace of God is, or it is not. That it was so fully revealed in Christ matters immeasurably in teaching and interpretation, and the Spirit becomes present in personal and public devotional experiences by which we are saved and healed. But one either has core belief superior to the anxieties of guilt, or one does not.

The most authentic communications of core belief are spontaneous; indeed, they have quite often been more evident in facial expression than in words. Until recently, this failure to be verbalized had meant that Black belief systems received no scholarly consideration, either as culture or as theology. Yet ensuing chapters reveal that many folk expressions contain theological content. There is every reason to believe that people intuitively choose the songs, for instance, that provide the type of nourishment they need. In other words, Soul theology has been built with an eye to the needs of the believers. The singing system, therefore, is what it is because of what it has already done for millions of oppressed people.

A final word about core beliefs concerns what some scholars see as their rigidity. Sara Little, an authority on belief and Christian education, sums it up by saying that core beliefs "are reshaped only at great cost. . . ." She expresses the hope that they may be "developed in such a way that drastic or traumatic shifts are unnecessary, and that core beliefs can serve as filters or organizing centers for free growth" (1983, 18–19). Dr. Little goes on to suggest that belief is most helpful when confirmed in human activities. Her goals for belief include growth towards conformity to reality and to higher ethical principles.

Soul folk would be the last to deny the need for growth in one's beliefs, but core beliefs among them are viewed much more positively. Rather than being considered rigid, core beliefs are seen as a necessary anchor in life's storm. Without formal or sophisticated rationale, the oppressed people holding core beliefs tend to assume that God takes good care of them. Old prayers thanked God that "He woke me up this morning, clothed in my right mind" (sane and emotionally balanced, despite the cruelties experienced). What looks like rigidity to some people is seen in the ghetto as stability and strength.

The significance of the contrast becomes clear when analyzing the core beliefs so common in the Soul community. The following cases illustrate that the affirmations believed to be so healing and empowering stem from lofty visions of God. These indigenous but informal views of God resemble the faith that Little and others consider the goal of the belief process. By contrast, the Soul view of the world and its Creator *starts* from these affirmations. The faith of Soul folk begins with belief in a God who preserves them through perpetual and undeserved pain and suffering.

The wholeness and emotional balance implied in Black core beliefs need to be defined. While Soul folk would hardly dream of such a detailed description, there are concrete ways to describe this goal of mental and spiritual health.

First of all, emotional balance enables people to function at full capacity physically, intellectually, emotionally, and spiritually. Secure despite hardships and traumatic change, they adapt as situations demand, using self-control and discipline, and keeping their own purpose and identity. Emotional balance involves the self-confidence that makes possible humor and comfortable relationship to others. When alone they are secure, balanced in lifestyle, and effective in independent or cooperative roles. This happy state includes the ability to compete where appropriate and to compromise without feeling undone.

Ideal balance empowers people to affirm their own gender, ethnicity, and peculiar personhood and still be other-centered and self-giving. They are dependable without being rigid and capable of expressing and controlling emotion. The bottom line of their balance is that they have a positive sense of relationship to God and God's creation, however stated or envisioned. Such an ideal state is the goal against which the effects of belief systems and world views will be examined. This book assumes that such healing can rightly be expected of a belief system.

A world view that functions as a basis for emotional balance must be recognized as theology. In fact, *all* theology might do well to be this serviceable. Just as the Sabbath observance was made for humanity, and not humanity for the Sabbath (Mark 2:27), so might also the so-called orthodox doctrine be required to serve human spiritual need first. It would, of course, glorify God in the process, just as does the Sabbath. But orthodoxy has not emphasized nearly enough God's ministry to human need, as compared with God's or the church's measure of conformity to tradition. The word of Jesus in the Mark account suggests his concern for people to be fed; he saw no glory for God or anyone else in hunger required by a rule that was backed only by narrow tradition. In emergencies, as Jesus suggested, even the most orthodox were willing to water animals and avoid material loss, but they criticized him for healing human beings on the holy day (Luke 13:15). Likewise, Christianity, which has been so vociferous about salvation by grace, has in effect tried to make orthodox faith statements into a form of works. The impact of grace is lost when conformity of words is the main concern. Theology at its best must be an elaboration of the Word that is revered because it gives life, serves needs, and heals minds and bodies by way of a powerful core belief or trust in God.

Beginning with core belief or functional world view raises the possibility of a whole new method and motivation for doing theology. It reverses the sequence of Western theological thought, which has customarily started with a corpus of doctrinal assumptions and reasoned deductively from them. The Soul method has innocently and informally, even unintentionally, built its "summa theologica" from Bible verses both close to earlier (African and Old Testament) wisdom and known to help cheer and heal souls under siege. However, the Soul system is not therefore unalterably opposed to deductive reasoning from principles. In fact, the affirmations on which soul folk have depended were invariably drawn from the Bible. The point is that even Bible principles were selected, formally or informally, according to the way they functioned. Blacks worked more naturally from experience as the criterion of meaning, and practical images as its symbolic vehicles. They built a system now recognized as both coherent and functional that might be called an inductive system.

The question arises immediately whether this system is in fact inductive. To the extent that the folk method starts with revealed wisdom assumed to be beyond question, it approximates deductive methods. Thinking about God, like all thought, begins with assumptions. Aquinas knew that one must believe something before one can think at all, inductively or deductively. The book of Hebrews stated pointedly that they who would come to God must first believe that he is (11:6). It is not possible to start from zero and work inductively; there is no zero point.

The folk system provides a minimal core belief that is passed on to children without their awareness of when it was learned. The Ashanti say that nobody shows a child the sky; they mean that the culture plants God-consciousness in children virtually at birth. The functionally developed belief system associated with the inductive method therefore begins deductively.

However, the inductive or functional method is not totally divorced from the deductive or revelatory system. The Word revealed to the prophets was influenced by particular times, places, and conditions. Later interpreters may have used it deductively, but the original message arose from the prophets' familiarity with surrounding life. Placing ideas in the scholarly systems of theology, then, is valid only after testing them in the laboratory of common life, not simply after answering abstract questions.

In moving inductively from experience, Black folk process used life's details as effective bearers of symbolic meaning.

Their method resembled most "primitive" cultures. Tribal societies almost universally preserved history and wisdom in animal stories and other types of narrative. The custodians of the common life knew no better way to socialize the young than to tell theologically significant stories. The fact that stories were art and not argument did not concern them; they knew stories made indelible impressions on memory and had a calculated impact on behavior. In other words, the African society assumed a functional intent for theology, and in America the rule has persisted by intuition. Thus no child was considered equipped or even fit for life who was not steeped in this oral tradition, which, though it was eminently theological, was not concerned with defense against intellectual attack. Apologetic was not at issue, nor was intellectual respectability. The doctrine-in-narrative form instead used familiar people and animals as symbols with which to improve the quality of life. No other purpose was conceivable.

While classical Western Christianity developed through defending abstract challenges from Greco-Roman intellectualism, the religion of Africa and Black America was shaped by the struggle to survive in a meaningful way. The challenge of survival still appears to have wide relevance to human need. If the medium is the message, then the folk or narrative process as opposed to the intellectual or academic process is likewise more relevant. The narrative approach would view the Bible as oral tradition with all the awesome authority this entails in folk culture. But the interpretation of the Bible would be relieved of the deadly abstractions of literalism. Just as tales were told for their value to the common life, so their interpretation involved no need for scientific historical verification. Narrative method requires that the story be told, not torn apart in analysis, and trusted in as core belief, not admired as science.

Soul theology speaks also to the idea of the canon, the corpus of narratives deemed worthy of memory and transmission to succeeding generations. There is little question that the most popular tales in African tradition were told for their usefulness and effectiveness. Likewise, the popularity of Moses, the emancipator, and Jesus, the suffering Son of God and link to heaven, were themes chosen by African-Americans in the crucible of need. The tale-telling Black preacher and the repertoire of gospel songs still reflect real need, not categories of thought in a theological world far removed from real life. The theological implications of this selective process are great, and they could well be used to discipline the menu offered by pulpiteers of learning, whatever their culture.

Choosing the canon on the basis of need is not unique to Black folk process. Probably this was precisely what happened, on a formal basis, in the ancient church council's selection of the canon of the Bible. Some opposed the choice of Solomon's Song, but it was included because it had been used by God. Nor were the decisions to include the prophets made on the basis of some mystical wiretap. The excesses of bibliolatry (idolatry of written word) are relatively late, while the very credibility, perpetual popularity, and eternal significance of the Bible are rooted in historical applicability to the human condition.

Internal evidence from the biblical text also indicates that belief was tested in the laboratory of experience. Messages originally received in the sincerest search for divine truth were nevertheless later superseded as human hearing of the changeless God improved. Deut. 25:5-6 requires an already married brother to marry his brother's widow, but 1 Tim. 3:2 reveals that a man should be husband of one wife at a time. Ezekiel's worship concepts were at first wed to the cult of the temple at Jerusalem, but he learned from need that God must surely want the Law to be written on people's hearts (36:26). He thereby laid the foundation for faith to remain whole throughout the Diaspora. God is always moving to meet needs and moving persons (by revelation) to respond to those needs.

Of course, too much attention can be given to perceived need. One can be so caught up in selfish concerns that one will misinterpret both biblical and current revelation, as did American slave owners. They quoted Paul out of context to defend their demonic system, forgetting his pointed conclusion that there is only one master, God (Eph. 6:9).

Another test of adequate data base involves asking whose needs determine the choice of Bible passage. It is a monstrous arrogance to consider the needs of supposed masters while ignoring the needs of the slaves and all others. The highest good for the largest number may not be the most profound goal of Christian ethics and theology, but it is certainly a minimum. Inductive theology at its best seeks to reach the needs of the whole of humanity, even while it seeks a belief system that meets the needs of persons one by one.

Finally, the folk process involves the whole idea of biblical authority. Oral tradition has never failed to sway its community. Assumed to be given by the Deity to the ancestors for the clear purpose of supporting and maintaining the extended-family society, the folk tradition brooked no opposition. Concerted social coercion made dissenters all the more unlikely. One would hardly want to return to enforcement used in primitive society, but the motives of the belief system and the momentum of the respect given it are still intuitively alive in the Black community. Crucial tales of an accurate but orally appropriated Holy Bible are heard and internalized at an early age. The meanings often last, regardless of academic erosions. This momentum is not a tribute to abstract authority of the sort that declares 'My Bible says right here in black and white. . . ." It reflects, rather, the liveliness and power with which the tales were told, and the interest with which they were and are habitually heard. Even more, it reflects the traditional authority and Christian authenticity of the teller.

In summary, the methods suggested in the case studies reported are belatedly recognized as efforts to regain some of these very same methods, meanings, and values in a clinical setting. However, the most important purpose of this volume, theologically speaking, is to identify and test the oral tradition comprising the survival kit of Soul theology, the body of folk beliefs of Black Christians. The authors of this book have tried to focus on maintaining and sharing a marvelous corpus of affirmations from the Bible. Beliefs have been assessed for their impact on the lives of the believers and their possible significance for persons of whatever culture.

From another perspective, this book can be said to to be a first effort at assembling the theology of Blacks. The approach differs from the liberation theme of Black theology to date, with its emphasis on social and political ends. Soul theology speaks pastorally, recording the all-too-often unspoken and quite informal belief system of the masses of ordinary people in the Black community. It spells out the beliefs used for survival, but it also collects the theological yield of the yearnings of a stolen people to be free and whole under God. It ceases at last to take for granted whatever sustenance came from the beliefs, and it reverently and respectfully examines the various forms that add up to a coherent system worthy of the respect of all humankind. It is especially deserving of the pride and understanding of the descendants of its ancestral authors.

The ten affirmations dealt with here are not in themselves the final word on Black folk theology. However, they do reflect the faith and strength of millions who embraced similar affirmations. The inductive method employed here scans the entire culture of Blacks for just such affirmations, respecting their folk wisdom in selection. The ten affirmations embodied in the following thirty cases illustrate this faith's healing powers. This is not a scientific data base for final proof of the effect of these core beliefs. However, these affirmations and the folk system of belief they comprise persist even today among a people that has survived despite predictions to the contrary. The fact that this people is a growing influence in the world, both spiritually and intellectually, speaks well for their inductive folk method.

It is significant, however, that this collection of the survival affirmations of Black folk does not resemble the set of beliefs that either conservative or liberal Christian traditions hold important. *Not one* standard text from supposedly learned theology deals at any length with these beliefs. Truly, the system these affirmations represent does not parallel anything currently classified as systematic theology. As a working body of beliefs, they have been overlooked altogether.

This neglect cannot be lightly regarded. It affirms that the inductive folk method, or the survival-based, need oriented method is probably just as novel to "respectable" theology as has been proposed. But more importantly, if the tree is known by its fruit, this method has a most outstanding theological yield to its credit. Sensitive writers from *Christianity Today* to *Christian Century* report in unison that they find high value systems in the most unlikely places in Black communities. In fact, this method and its yield are so impressive that they raise searching questions about the methods that have produced the variety of well-established theologies. Is human need this various, or is the diversity a matter of fads in abstract intellectualism? Did Paul's laudable endeavor to interpret Christian faith to Greco-Roman culture put too permanent and pervasive an imprint on theological method? Should someone have explored long before now the theological method of Old Testament oral tradition? Perhaps it should not totally replace but at least supplement and correct the mission-by-mental-appeal approach with which Paul enlarged the borders of the faith. To say the least, much can be explored in this new but old way of doing theology intuitively, assuming belief must heal and help the believer as well as honor the God of all creation and of grace.

As the authors reflected on how truly unique this folk system might be, it suddenly occurred to them that the closest parallels were the widely known catalogs of African praise names for God. The body of Black belief, in Africa and in the United States, largely centers on the attributes of God that impinge on human experience. The facts of that experience make up the data base of this impromptu and inductive theology. Traditionally emphasized topics like "the nature of being," or "revelation and reason," or the technicalities of the Trinity are not so easy to encounter in experience, so they largely escape the purview of the more primitive systems. All of the affirmations of the Black belief system are more focused on dealing with God and with life than with intellectual issues.

Theology surely needs in time to solve such issues as reason and revelation, but Soul takes revelation for granted without being anti-intellectual. The primary concern of its "primitive" system is this mortal struggle. The vast majority of the Old Testament's theological affirmations had a similar purpose, probably because of the same kind of folk theological selectivity. Soul sisters and brothers therefore need to make no apologies for their insistence that beliefs be down to earth and work in real life.

The following cases suggest that one may very well become a more creative intellectual—a much better speculative theologian—if one has grown up in and grasped the more basic beliefs of Soul. At the beginning of each chapter, the affirmations are spelled out in almost sermonic terms. This is, after all, the best if not the only known way of verbalizing most of these powerful core beliefs.

2. The Providence of God

"And we know that God works in everything for good. . . ." (Rom. 8:28)

The most essential and inclusive of these affirmations of Black core beliefs is called *the Providence of God* in Western terms. Many Blacks may not have so precise a word for it, and they may not even know that the idea they cling to so naturally is called a doctrine. But in Africa and Afro-America, the most treasured and trusted word about our life here on earth is that God is in charge. This faith guarantees that everyone's life is worth living. The Bible passage that expresses it best is Paul's famous word to the Romans: "And we know that God works in everything for the good of those who love him and are called according to his plan."

In academic circles such an attitude may be called a "positive world view." It is the deep and sweeping assertion that the whole universe is friendly or benevolent, and that its Creator is able and willing to turn into good ends whatever may occur. Within Black culture this is a given, but to minds shaped in other cultures, it may seem like wishful thinking—an imagined comfort and escape from reality. However, among Soul folk it is a foundational and fruitful insistence on which all life and effort depend. There can be no final disproof of it, because the doctrine always refers to ultimate ends; the disbelievers and challengers simply have not waited long enough. Oppressed people are supported by the conviction that the very Lord of the universe has guaranteed that their lives will always be worth living.

The lens through which reality is seen is not rose colored and inclined to overlook offenses. The realism of the tradition is evident in spirituals like "Sometimes I Feel like a Motherless Child," or "Nobody Knows the Trouble I See." But the tradition holds that for every evil perpetrated against the believer God has either a counterbalancing good or else will squeeze from the evil itself a literal blessing. So the faithful constantly seek out hidden good, knowing that God does not explicitly will that evils should come or that divinely ordained freedom should be used to hurt others. God's plan is *good* for those who love their Creator and affirm that plan, whether individuals or whole groups.

God's Providence implies and includes an impressive array of other divine attributes that Western theological tradition has also established as doctrine. The chief of these is the sovereignty and/or Omnipotence of God (the unlimited control and power without which God could not turn evil designs to good ends, nor provide the necessities implicit in the very word Providence). It also involves omniscience, or all-knowingness. This quality is necessary for reading not only human need but mortal motives, as well as the divinely ordained sequels of cause and effect. Omniscience borders on another doctrine called predestination, which may be applied theoretically in widely varying degrees.

The warmest of the attributes called forth within Providence is the grace of God as giver of all good things, even when they are not deserved. It is supremely important to affirm this divine intent to give good gifts, although theologians fearing "cheap grace" circulate rumors resembling the contrary. Whether in Western or Afro-American tradition, belief in Providence and grace is essential to well-being. Since they are so loaded with meaning, these doctrines along with Omnipotence and omniscience will be treated in separate chapters despite a great deal of overlap.

The powerful positiveness and elaborateness of this belief system raises the question about how people in slavery acquired it. The answer lies in the cultural and religious equipment that Blacks brought with them to these shores. The preludes to the personal case studies presented in the rest of this work show that African culture held a well-developed world view expressed in traditional songs and tales, riddles and proverbs. Africans considered proverbs the horse on which all conversation rides, and they expressed their trust in Providence most clearly through this medium. The graphic details used in proverbs symbolize the goodness of centuries of African life and explain in part the cultural momentum that kept the belief system alive through following centuries of suffering.

For Africans, God's care extends to the details of everyday life. The Yoruba, the Anga, and others say, "It is God who drives away the flies for the cow who has no tail." The Ashanti state, "It is the Supreme Being who pounds fufu [a fibrous staple like hard potatoes] for the one without arms." In both cases, God works for good by providing life's essentials. This is the first and most obvious aspect of Providence.

However, like their enslaved descendents, traditional Africans did not claim this Providence in a naive vacuum. One proverb declares that God will not let the drum of slander sound, but it recognizes the existence of this evil nonetheless. Another proclaims that although we may not know exactly who they will be, God will always provide friends even in the worst of times. This condition called hard times is even more candidly faced in a Gonja (Northern Ghana) proverb: "God arranges things so that the leper's sandals break under the camelfoot bush." In the midst of problems as persistent as leprosy, God provides remedies such as the shrub that supplies fibers for the repair of sandals. This proverb brightens life by focusing on the fibers for repair rather than on the leprosy.

In the midst of death and other sorrows, the common life of the traditional African village is punctuated by joyous celebrations of God's care. They occur at planting and harvest, birth and marriage, and at death, the final stage in the cycle of the good life. God is seen to be at work even in death. The physical grave is not considered the end, since the "living dead" are constantly remembered, attended to, and consulted.

Africans imported for slavery managed to survive largely because they held onto their belief systems so tenaciously. They survived by praising God and being traditionally thankful for the goodness of life, even though they were in bondage. Their fixation on God's goodness was so great that they literally shouted about it. They could endure a lot of cruelty by focusing their attention on mental recollections or reruns of pleasant experiences considered blessings from God.

Their original determination to document the goodness of God and of life is still alive and well in traditional soul prayers. The providing Deity receives thanks in the morning for waking us up by "touching us with the finger of love" and for the fact that we were "clothed in our right minds." "Our bed was not our cooling board," and "we were able to pick and choose our own praying ground." This is surely the prime example of what the Apostle Paul meant when he said, "If there be any virtue, if there be any praise, think on these things" (Phil. 4:8). Soul folk contemplate God's smallest blessings so seriously that they rejoice at the very thought of God's care. And so they are healed by joy in the midst of pain; blessed because they literally count *all* their benefits.

Since this belief system underlies Black culture as a whole, it is nearly as manifest outside the churches as within them. Luke, the dope dealer in Chapter 1, expressed profound trust levels while in the most threatening of situations: facing his first long jail term. He casually cited and applied the doctrines of Providence and omniscience with a familiarity and accuracy born of long acquaintance. Nor was Lola Falana in that same chapter merely citing pious platitudes. Her belief applied adequately to a collection of perplexing problems. In the poetic prayers of Soul worship just cited, the Providence of God is no more concretely applied than in these situations completely outside the church. The doctrine literally lives and is leaned on in most facets of Black life.

That does not mean that street culture has no poetic expressions of its own. The very authentic breed of Soul songs called the blues abounds in its own affirmations of the goodness of life. The despair implied by the name blues is only valid "in the sense that there is no attempt to cover up reality" (Cone 1972, 140). Sometimes with and sometimes without the mention of God, the lyrics always affirm the ultimate goodness of human existence. One blues song admits that the singer is blue, but he declares he won't be blue always. He is sure that the sun will shine in his backdoor some day.

Similarly, B. B. King, a famous blues singer, sings a long litany of mistreatment by a woman and then declares, "There's got to be a better world. . . ."

This is not radically different from the sadder spirituals. "Sometimes I Feel like a Motherless Child" ends in a final affirmation: *"True Believer* a long way from home." Another spiritual says, "Nobody knows the trouble I see. . . . [That is] Nobody knows but Jesus. *Glory Hallelujah!"* In both blues and spirituals, the singer can stand to keep on living and trying because of this vision of a positive end, the outcome of Providence.

Comparable belief in the Providence of God and the goodness of life can be found in both Old and New Testaments. The manna in the wilderness (Exod. 16:15, 35) and the inexhaustible food supply of the widow at Zarephath (1 Kings 17) all testify to God's Providence. Jesus declared that God is waiting to give us good gifts (Matt. 7:11) and that God's care includes such minutiae as the numbering of the very hairs on our heads (Matt. 10:30). The definitive act of God that launched the entire Hebrew-Christian tradition was the providential act of deliverance known as the Exodus. God worked for good in the Red Sea.

Occasionally Soul folk confront the question of the proof of Providence. The simple answer, of course, is that it cannot be proved, but neither can it be disproved. Belief in Providence is a matter of faith—a fruitful and life-supporting hypothesis. If you believe it, you can survive until providential deliverance comes, and it always does. If you deny it, you have lost the basis of hope. There is no reason to continue struggling if this life is not and will never become worth living.

A lengthier answer to the question of proving God's Providence points to the exact places where the believer sees God's work for good. God is provident in three "l"s: the limits, the leavings, and the last end.

God is provident in the limits set or built into life. There is a sense in which all our lives enjoy protection from extremes similar to the limit God placed on Satan's assaults on Job: "Thus far, and no further: you may not take his life" (2:6). Satan had to ask permission and remain within the bounds of that grant. Luke the dope dealer expresssed belief in a parallel limit when he declared that God would not let more come upon him than he could deal with. He was, likely, paraphrasing a gospel song, "He Knows Just How Much You Can Bear," based on 1 Cor. 10:13, written in the depression by Roberta Martin. The Providence of God guarantees the goodness of life by placing ultimate limits on the impact of evil—slavery or holocaust notwithstanding.

God's Providence is also evident in what Delia Lindsay King, the mother of Martin Luther King, Sr., called the "leavings." The senior King learned this phrase from his mother and preached about it many years ago, but he maintained and repeated it even after losing two sons and his beloved wife, slain at the organ during Sunday worship. It was an unforgettable testimony of faith to hear him still say that life *always* has enough left to make it worth the living. One person says the glass is half empty, but another sees it as half full and praises God. Those who complain to God about what they don't have are forgetting that their very breath is a gift from God. After tragedy there is always something—life, air, or "a reasonable portion of health and strength" (phrase from a Soul prayer)—left to praise God for. Our provident God always leaves us something on which to keep going.

Third, God's Providence is evident in the last end. It may appear that the forces of evil and suffering will get the best of us and our world. But if we are tempted to feel that trusting is useless and righteousness is in vain, we must remember the last end. God is guaranteed to win over the hosts of evil. Like a baseball game, evil may hit bases-loaded homers and trap us in deadly double plays, but this is only an early inning. God's hosts will outscore evil and save the game. In the end God shall reign forever and ever (Rev. 22:5). Hallelujah! The Providence of God works in everything for good, all the way to the eschatological end.

God's Providence is graphically illustrated in the story of Joseph, which climaxes the very first book in the Bible. All the rest of Genesis can be said to lead up to Joseph's testimony to God's Providence in the story which is now recalled.

After the burial of their father in the family plot, Joseph's older brothers returned to Egypt. During the dusty journey they recalled the advice of their late father to beg their brother Joseph's forgiveness. They sent a letter to Joseph and followed it up with an appointment in his prime minister's chambers. Their speeches went something like this:

"First of all, we want you to know that we admire you greatly. We feel bad about selling you into slavery, but you have borne it with an amazingly calm and even spirit. We understand that you were badly treated because you would not play games with Potiphar's wife, but you didn't become embittered. When you were unjustly sentenced to Pharaoh's prison, even this did not crush your spirit. In fact, you converted your sentence into a ministry that landed you in your present position.

"Now, of course, you have held this high office many years, and this too has not turned your head. When we came to you during the famine, you were most gracious, and we are most grateful. But we feel like Daddy did; it was partly out of respect for him. Now that he is gone, we are on our own and scared. We feel like chickens running before a hawk in an open field. It's only a matter of time before you will get us. So we have come to fall at your feet and beg forgiveness. Please, Brother Joseph, have mercy on us! We are your willing servants for the rest of our days."

Joseph had been listening with bowed head, while he wept a

little. When he saw them on their knees before him, he asked them to get right up. He said with deep feeling, "Am I the place of God? Don't be afraid of me! Now as to your confessions, of course I know that you plotted viciously against me, and I came close to being killed at your hands. There is no hatred quite like that which sometimes arises between brothers. I have no illusions about your intentions at the time, but even though you meant it to me for evil, God meant it to me for good."

Many Blacks could testify to the same faith. "I never get too worried, because I know that God works in *every*thing for good. Life looks pretty bad at times, but I have learned that when one door is slammed shut, God reserves the right to open a larger one for me. My God sets a limit on the things you can do to believers and always leaves some way for them to keep going. I declare unto you that the last end is always worth all the trouble we have been through. I *know* that God works in everything for good, and reserves the right to squeeze a final blessing out of *any*thing." This is the very cornerstone of the Soul system of belief that has kept many Blacks alive and creative regardless of hardships.

Consider now three real cases that illustrate the vast impact of this folk doctrine and biblical affirmation of Providence when applied in therapy. Names and details have been changed to protect the patients, but the essentials are documentary.

Case 1

Our first case involves Tom, whose record-breaking series of misfortunes had very nearly convinced him that God was anything but provident. The only trouble was that if life really was too hard to be worth living, the logical thing to do was commit suicide.

Tom was a twenty-eight-year-old professional. He came to the office of the therapist detached and masking deep pain. His wife and baby had just moved out of their home, and this had left him utterly shattered. His feelings and his intellect were disconnected, and his report was given in the third person, as if he were speaking of someone else. He described the whole affair in flat tones. The empty and dispassionate objectivity that he affected helped him avoid the pain. "I work and think, but I don't feel. I'm *afraid* to feel." He was quite correct about this, for his real feelings would have taken him far beyond his beliefs and professional inhibitions. He feared his emotional response to the mistreatment received would have been dangerously explosive, so he placed his emotions in limbo, bottling up his hostilities and fears.

He had worked all his life to become a good person and to make for someone an ideal husband and father. Despite being battered and alienated in early years, he had dared to dream, and now all his dreams were dashed. He seemed incapable of envisioning a fresh start. He had taken all he thought he could, and his visit to the therapist was a sign of despair. It was as if he were saying, "I dare you to show me why I should not try suicide again and this time make sure I don't fail." It was his last desperate effort to find a straw of hope.

Tom's case history was strewn with brutalities received from his family. In the teen years he had suffered long periods of literal solitary confinement for trivial and even imaginary infringements. He had naturally responded with a very low self-image and continuous efforts to deserve his supposed parents' love. Then, at sixteen, when a relative had broken the contract of silence, he had discovered that those were not his natural parents after all. The rest of his life had been absorbed in the search for a family that would really love him.

Ironically, all his efforts yielded little; his newly located blood relatives were no better than the ones who had reared him. His latest wife had rejected him and exploited his vulnerability, so that the safety and support of the family he had always sought had once again been snatched away from him. The therapist knew he could not change any of the given conditions in Tom's world, nor did he think that doing so would have helped at this late stage. The change had to come from within Tom.

After thorough analysis, the course of treatment prescribed led through several stages to the bottom line of core belief. First, his emotions were freed so that he could express them safely in a supportive and therapeutic environment. Then he honestly confronted the hazards and the high cost of his hostile, angry refusals to forgive. The therapist heightened Tom's awareness that cruel family members were sick, too, and that they sinned against themselves even more than against him. The pain of their offenses led all the way back to Tom's childhood and had to be released for his own good.

With the entire cast of heartless rejecters safely removed from the center of Tom's inner stage, the therapist began to focus on the beliefs by which Tom had managed to survive. He was helped also to see what beliefs had all but destroyed them. He was then guided through long listening sessions of supportive Bible materials. The therapist provided sermon tapes on passages from Job, Hebrews, and Romans. Tom could identify with Job's sense of unspeakable loss. The discussion of faith in verses 1 and 6 of Hebrews 11 affirmed the centrality of hope and belief in God's presence. A supremely important tape on Rom. 8:28 emphasized that God does not directly will the evils that befall us but reserves the right to work for good even inside the processes of human freedom and cruelty. This tape referred back to Joseph who in Genesis 50 said the same sort of thing: "You meant it to me for evil, but God meant it to me for good." The name of the doctrine in these taped affirmations was the Providence of God.

With all these positive messages about life and God, Tom began to feel much better about himself, and he was able to stop taking his exwife's weaknesses and apparent savagery personally. He determined that she was indeed largely responsible for the final failure of their family, but the fault lay in her weakness and lifelong family conditioning, not in raw malice on her part. Tom now found it possible to respect himself for having done all that he could do, and also calmly to forgive her understandable limitations, notwithstanding the harm they had brought him. Above all, it was obvious that even in the midst of this crushing divorce, he could see God working for good.

His next step was to trust this provident God for the future—to affirm and build on the blessings that God had just squeezed out. It was a chance to start all over again. This time he would understand himself and his place in God's world a lot better. He would not repeat the errors he made in his previous and sincere but misguided attempts to establish a family. Now he was enjoying far greater reserves of energy and creativity, and he would face a future far brighter than any he had ever seen before. The provident God had been there and acting throughout his life, but now Tom had come to trust him, and that made all the difference in the world.

Case 2

Darlene saw herself as both worthless and defenseless. But despite all the batterings she had received, God had been providently at work in her life, and there was far more in store for her than she had ever dared to dream.

At age twenty-four, she had nearly been committed for the third time in a psychiatric facility. Deeply depressed, very anxious and "nervous" (her word), and utterly afraid, Darlene was perpetually horrified that people might reject her. She cried almost incessantly and was afraid to be alone despite her desperate shyness. Her case history easily explained how she came to her condition.

Darlene had been removed from her natural home at age eight, after having been beaten and raped almost daily. As a ward of the court, she had fared a little better in terms of physical safety, but no better in emotional support. Always seeking to be accepted and loved, she started going to church on her own at age fifteen. Just when this new experience was beginning to provide a glimmer of hope that the church was loving and strong enough to care for her, she was molested in the parking lot of the church. Five years later, two men broke into her apartment and beat and raped her.

About this time she began seeking protection from molesting males through marriage. However, again, her plight failed to improve. When her inevitable symptoms of massive depression reappeared, her husband simply had her twice committed to the state hospital. He apparently enjoyed her deep dependence on him, but he could not fulfill the responsibility. He expected the therapist to sign the papers and put her away the third time, but Darlene's pattern providentially was changed.

This therapist saw within all her efforts to improve her situation a tiny spark of dogged, healthy determination. Darlene had a profound and wholesome refusal to accept conclusively her understandable doubts about the power and Providence of God. Her worst doubts were not about God but about herself. She had internalized much from her early experiences of violence and rejection, so she had all but succumbed to the conviction that this living hell was all she deserved. Her husband was happy to feed his own ego with her helplessness, and he evidenced some disappointment when she was permitted to sign up for outpatient treatment instead of hospitalization.

Darlene's recovery was as startlingly rapid as her history had been shockingly brutal. Within a short time she calmly informed her husband that any sickness still in the family belonged to him. She offered him two options: he could accept the healed Darlene and start recovering from his own need of her dependency, or he could get out of her life altogether. What had this healer done in seventeen sessions that other hospitals and professionals had failed to do?

First, Darlene and the therapist placed her problems in proper perspective. They decided that her illness started not at the moment when those early horrors had occurred; rather she had become sick only when she started believing these experiences were accurate indexes of her own worth and of the level of care God had for her. Up to that point, the assaults were only a reflection of the illness of others. She was helped to see that since these incidents were beyond her control, they were also beyond her responsibility. On the other hand, she was accountable for letting herself believe what all this seemed to imply about herself and her God.

Several methods helped erase old doubts and reinforce her residue of faith. First, she was assigned fail-safe tasks. At the completion of each, she was led to recall and celebrate her successes, and she was given assurance of her ability to repeat them. She was guided into relaxation and meditation during which she fed her deepest consciousness on hymns, spirituals, and gospel songs by artists such as Mahalia Jackson. This great singer had triumphed over amazing handicaps and specialized in singing affirmations of faith in God's Providence with a warm and convincing authenticity that was very healing.

Darlene began to see Providence not only as helping her resist assaults, but also as preparing her to perform respected tasks in the wider world. She had some marvelous place in the plan of God, and, like all God's offspring, she was special. She read repeatedly the parable in Matthew 25 that illustrates the obligation to use personal talents (25:14–30). With this encouragement she found a new job, her very first position above the skills level of a kitchen helper. Her amazing shift in circumstances confirmed her growing belief that God really was at work in her life and exerting unlimited power and wisdom on her behalf. She marvelled at her own good fortune, and she celebrated and freely expressed her newfound certainty of the Providence of God.

Case 3

Sarah was in her mid-fifties and had rarely considered God and Providence when she first sought help. She was beginning to get a better vision of herself and her worth in God's sight when suddenly the blow fell. Her husband, a man in his early

sixties, left her for a much younger woman. He had been se-
cretly saving money for this escape for some time. Even the
minimal crumbs of acceptance that he had given her between
criticisms now turned out to have been false.

Sarah was still reeling from the painful realities of her life
when her estranged husband was just as suddenly brought
back home to her care. He had suffered a heart attack and a
light stroke, and his thirty-four-year-old apartment mate had
abandoned him. The man was so completely crushed that if
Sarah had refused his feebly stated request, he would have had
little or no reason left to live. She could see this, and she could
not say no.

Her course of therapy included listening to affirmations from
the Bible and several stories. The story that seemed to reach her
best was Hans Christian Andersen's "Ugly Duckling." At the
end of the story, the slow, strange-looking bird is found to be
not a duck at all, but a baby swan. Sarah learned to affirm the
deep beauty of her own that God had given her.

Sarah also learned that she was a worthwhile person with or
without a husband. Intrinsic personal value was a gift from
God, not from any human being, including her husband. This
fresh awareness curbed her habit of being a self-made doormat.
A command or affirmation from the Bible that she heard over
and over in treatment was, "Thou shalt love the Lord thy God
. . . and thy neighbor as thyself" (Matt. 22:37–39).

Sarah's newfound self-esteem inevitably removed the cover
from old hidden anger and frustration. The real Sarah was free
to stand up and be identified, and her deeply repressed hostilities were allowed to surface. This could have been dangerous,
but here, again, a story became important. The injustices suffered by Joseph and his faith in God's ability to turn evil into
good ends (Gen. 50) spoke to Sarah's situation. She discovered
that Joseph was never actually powerless, even when his brothers sold him into slavery, because God was planning to bring
not only justice but also great blessing out of Joseph's misfortune. With this expectation, Joseph could wait in calm dignity

for God's deliverance. Through this story Sarah was freed from her own sense of powerlessness in the face of injustice and oppression, and the wound of her repressed anger opened and healed. She could say, with Joseph, "You meant it to me for evil, but God meant it to me for good."

Sarah cared for her semi-invalid husband without bitterness, giving thanks to God that she now had a place of complete acceptance at last. She was content with the new Sarah. Clearly her husband was paying dearly for his misdeeds, but Sarah was free to help him back to wholeness. Instead of feeling powerless and exploited, she maintained her growing self-esteem and looked for the blessings God would extract from it all. She was able to smile when speaking of the whole affair, and she gave the impression that life for her was more satisfying than it had been for a long, long time. It was not impossible that the Providence of God had planned a better relationship for them than they had ever dreamed of in the past.

Our lives are spent in a crucible of human freedom. People have the power to hurt as well as help each other. At times some people receive nothing but suffering, and for no imaginable reason. In the sickness of spirit this often causes, it is good to know that there are individuals and communities with a talent for stimulating in the crushed and discouraged the healing core belief that, in the Providence of God, bad news is never the final news. For those who love their Maker and seek to follow the divine plan for their lives, a good end is certain. The last movement in the symphony of life is always worth waiting for, and God guarantees this finale no matter what the prelude.

3. The Justice of God

"For whatsoever a man soweth, that shall he also reap." (Gal. 6:7)

God Is Just; this is the second affirmation of the religion under-girding much of Black life. God is caring and provident, but God is also fair and impartial. This important doctrine is not strange to Western Christian thought, either within or outside theological circles. The whole Hebrew-Christian tradition was launched on ethical monotheism, the idea that there is only one true God, and this Deity requires ethical accountability. As the prophet Micah declared, "And what doth the Lord require of thee, but to do justly, and to love mercy, and walk humbly with thy God?" (6:8) Western secular legal theory holds with equal certainty that if God is not just, then all their efforts through the centuries have been in vain. In a word, civilization itself, not just stereotypical "law and order," is vitally dependent on the core belief in the justice of God.

This affirmation is obviously relevant and applicable in almost every phase of Western intellectual as well as legal and ethical life. In the culture of the privileged classes and the power elite, enthusiasm for this doctrine results from a vision of God as enforcer or guarantor of the status quo. God threatens with justice those who break the social contract, raining retribution on those who dare to contradict the common code, which favors the class on top. However, this same divine quality is the hope of the have-nots. Justice is the limit placed on exploitation; it is the vengeance and vindication without which their lowly lives would have little meaning. God's holiness and righteousness, synonyms for justice, are the basis for all guilty conscience, whatever the sin and among whatever sector of the population. It is hard to visualize any ethical decision where this doctrine has no relevance.

Divine justice impinges on the thought of the nonbeliever as well as the devout. It underlies the intensity of the atheist's or the agnostic's concern for humane principles. For instance, the undeserved suffering of children can be used as an argument against God's existence. Nonbelievers maintain that if there were a God, that Deity would be just and would refuse to allow such a patent denial of fairness. Again, many skeptics choose the bleak wastes of alienation from God on the basis of a misguided picture of God's justice. They accept the notion that the Creator and Sustainer of all life promotes justice that requires the eternal fires of a burning hell. This is understandably repugnant to their thoughtful concerns and sensibilities.

Fortunately, the justice of God can be viewed more positively. It undergirds every crusade for equity and human betterment within the Judeo-Christian era. Social activists of every generation, including a wide spectrum of present proponents of the social relevance of the gospel, have all proclaimed the justice of God and depended on it for their validation. The nature of God does indeed demand radical changes in the established order.

Providing an alternative to both atheists and a hell-fire view of retribution are millions of people who find meaning in their lives in the certainty of divine justice. At this point Black belief finds it greatest commonality with the souls of Western and in fact all cultures. Of course Blacks seek a more intensive application of social justice, and they believe the God of justice is literally on the side of the oppressed. This, along with their sufferings caused by injustice, explains their more energetic efforts to bring about equal opportunity. However, an additional motivation comes from the fact that belief in God's justice also confers meaning on their struggles in the interim, keeping them sane in the midst of crushing absurdities. In the end, one must know that no oppression goes unpunished and no sacrificial suffering goes unnoticed and unrewarded. The just God who is no respecter of persons gives none the power to trample the rights of others with impunity. Thus, the final judgment day feared by some becomes cause for the celebration of vindication and victory for the victims of history's most glaring injustices. One dare not suggest that this meaning and comfort conferred through God's justice are the unique possession of any special group or class, since all persons see themselves as oppressed one way or another.

In Black culture, belief in God's justice may be documented as easily in the street as in the church. In the early days of her first stage career, the late Alberta Hunter, grand dame of contemporary blues, wrote a song illustrating this. Written to be sung by Bessie Smith, it dealt with a woman who had been thrown out by her lover. In her blue cries of pain she sings a social protest based on a folk doctrine of justice, which helps her remain balanced despite her desperation:

You treat me wrong; you drove me from yo' do' [door].
You treat me wrong; you drove me from yo' do'.
But the Good Book say you gonna reap what you sow.

This declaration of God's justice sounds almost like revenge by black magic, but its real function was to give a heartbroken, helpless woman a way to make sense of her powerless existence—a means of stamping on her days of the label, "Still Worth the Living."

The certainty of justice is not restricted to personal comfort in frustration. Its wisdom appears when there is no pressing personal need whatever, only sympathy for some other person suffering abuse. For example, a group of Black postal clerks is on lunch break. One brother finishes his sandwich and volunteers to regale the gang with tales of his exploits among women. His crew is hardly puritanical, but at the same time, they all sense that he is being downright vicious. An undercurrent of resistance and criticism builds up in their minds. Suddenly it bursts out in one word by a usually quiet fellow: "Payday!" On the blocks where they live, this word says it all: in the economy of God, there are wages (repayment) for such injustices.

Street folk may not mention God in all their references to justice, but everyone in the culture is likely to know who is behind the reality of justice. Sometimes they say, "Chickens come home to roost," a phrase widely publicized when Malcolm X tactlessly connected it with the John F. Kennedy assassination. The saying is built into Black culture. Whether Christian or Muslim or neither, the justice Malcolm X hinted at is all but universally recognized in the Black ghetto.

Perhaps the best-known and most frequently used folk phrase for this belief is the popular proverb, "What goes around comes around." Quoted in an infinite variety of situations, it always declares that life is lived in an inexorable system of accountability. No person can expect to sidestep the results of her or his actions; the consequences are as inevitable as the agricultural law of identical harvest. "God is not mocked, for whatsoever a man soweth, that shall he also reap" (Gal. 6:7).

The amazing popularity of justice among Blacks does not stem from their assigning it to other groups while evading its meaning for their own lives. They know that they, too, will be judged. But there can be no doubt that this justice is celebrated for quite different reasons: "It applies to the big league sinners who oppress me, even more than it applies to me." A slave narrative cited in *Black Belief* illustrates the basis for virtually getting happy over the very existence of hell:

We was scart of ol' Solomon and his whip. . . . He didn't like for us Niggers to pray either. We never heared of no church, but we was prayin' in the cabins. We'd set on the floor an' pray with our heads down low and sing low, but if Solomon heared, he'd come and beat on the wall with the stock of his whip. He'd say, "I'll come in there and tear the hides off you backs." . . . I know that Solomon is burnin' in hell today, and it pleasures me to know it (1975, page 16).

The spiritual "I Gotta Shoe" echoed this same joy about the afterlife as a place to straighten out the imbalances in the accounts of this life. With typical African indirection, the lyrics declared innocently, "When I git to heaven, gonna put on my shoes, and gonna shout all over God's heaven." Slaves thus safely voiced their protest that masters did not provide shoes in this life nor allow slaves to shout in church as the Spirit led them. However, in the ultimate state of things—in heaven—both of these gross evils would be corrected.

The song's chorus shifted to the other final destination. "Everybody talkin' 'bout heaven ain't a-goin' there, heaven, heaven, gonna shout all over God's heaven." With veiled language slaves announced that their masters were booked for hell. In the mind of the thinking slave, there was no such thing as a really good master, so they all had confirmed reservations.

African traditional religion had held no concept of hell. Once in this country, however, slaves adapted to the prevailing religion. They recognized that masters were theologically correct about the existence of hell, since there had to be a proper place for masters to finish reaping what they had sowed. Fire and brimstone were strange and novel but wonderfully capable of giving masters what they deserved.

This deep belief in the justice of God cannot be traced to missionaries whom the masters provided to teach about hell. The afterlife of fire and brimstone only dramatized in new detail the implementation of a divine justice known and trusted in Africa. In both Africa and America, the doctrine of justice was taught most effectively in oral tradition, by parents, grandparents, and the extended family or intimate community.

The Galatian text about reaping and sowing took hold so quickly among the slaves only because the "Law of Identical Harvest" had been established long since in the African mindset. The Yoruba people expressed it this way: "To sow is difficult, to reap is free; what you sow today is what you reap tomorrow." They had a succinct and powerfully meaningful name for God: Adekedajo, the silent active judge (Mitchell 1975, 71, 85). One of their proverbs was a prayer that petitions God to preserve the unjust enemy's health (especially his senses), so that the inevitable punishment due from a just God can be felt to the fullest. Then there is appended one small request: "Lord, let me be living and looking when the sentence is carried out." One knows that God is just, but one would rather see its results than simply believe.

Congregations of all cultures laugh heartily at this prayer, especially the last part. It is the high humor of self-recognition, the prayer of all classes, cultures, and generations. The ancient psalmist stated the same sentiment: "I had fainted unless I had believed to see the goodness of the Lord in the land of the living" (27:13). There is no cry here for petty vengeance; the healthy psyche of the just individual simply has to know that the flourishing of the wicked can only be for a season, and that God is not mocked with their ill-won successes. One's righteous efforts are therefore not rendered meaningless.

Within this life, questions about justice will remain. No finite soul can claim to have seen justice in every case. Neither can we expect to be in a position to monitor all God's just actions. Mere mortals must be content to see only some divine justice, and not even all of that right away. Some will become clear many years later and some only in the afterlife. A religious cross section of the American South unites today in singing a hymn that says, "Further along we'll understand why." A Black hymn with the same message is sung in even wider circles: "We will understand it better by and by."

This "by and by" or afterlife is indispensable to belief in the justice of God. The biblical figure Job, in trying circumstances, reportedly cried, "Though . . . worms destroy this body, yet in my flesh [my unique personhood] shall I see God: whom I shall see for myself . . ." (19:26–27). The theme of the book is the justice of God and the explanation of why good people suffer; significantly, Job's climactic affirmation of faith in God is, "Though He slay me, yet will I trust Him. . . ." (13:15).

The Apostle Paul echoed the book of Job by linking the two ideas of justice and afterlife. Paul ended his classic statement on eternal life by connecting it to the justice that is essential for meaningful human existence: "Therefore, my beloved brethren, be ye steadfast, unmovable, always abounding in the work of the Lord, forasmuch as ye know that your labor is not in vain in the Lord" (1 Cor. 15:58). Paul deals here with the bottom line: life is unbearable without such meaning. God's justice is essential to meaning even though it acts in the time frame of eternity. A Black gospel song sings triumphantly, "Then my living shall not be in vain." For all humanity, unless God is in fact just, life is indeed vain and not worth the living.

Slaves survived their shackles with a magnificent affirmation of the justice of God, contemplating the final judgment with celebration:

In that great gittin' up mornin' fare ye well, fare ye well.
In that great gittin' up mornin' fare ye well, fare ye well.

Of that same ultimate judgment they also sang, "Great day! the righteous marchin', great day, God's goin' to build up Zion's wall." The day has come when all humanity needs the certainty of God's justice as did the oppressed slaves and their descendants. None can afford to believe that God might be unjust.

The powerlessness of slaves has parallels throughout human life. Presidents of corporations and countries today wield power vastly larger than that of slaves. But the problems of pollution and inflation outweigh all efforts to solve them and thus show themselves even more powerful. The affluent parents of modern adolescents are often more powerless than those whose lives are compressed and disciplined by the pressures of poverty, provided minimal essentials are available. In a world where power in business and politics is dispersed among many individuals who may or may not be trustworthy, we have a fundamental need to know who is in control and to be able to trust that one to be fair and just. Otherwise, all struggle is meaningless. There is no segment of humanity immune to the need to affirm the justice of God.

The intellectual exercise of doubting God's justice may be healthy for a brief season, but if it lasts very long and goes very deep, it can lead to serious personality disorder, as the following cases illustrate.

Case 4

Carolyn, age thirty-five, believed God was just, and she was a lifelong crusader for the justice required by God. The only trouble was that she was unjust to herself, claiming too little of the good that she justly deserved. Fortunately, Carolyn knew she needed counseling. She was being battered physically and emotionally by her husband. Using theories from college psychology classes in her efforts to adjust to his uncommon emotional needs, she had sacrificed all reasonable concern for herself. Thus she offered less and less resistance to the abuse he heaped on her. She was losing all hope that even God wished anything better for her, so she began to emphasize in memory her smallest mistakes, unconsciously building a case for deserving her plight.

Her family background had stressed the Providence and justice of God, and in college she herself had been involved in student crusades for justice and equality. She simply refused to apply this same sense of justice to herself. Now into her second marriage, she felt this was her last chance to be married properly and retain her respectability in the eyes of God. Carolyn believed God would never forgive her for a second divorce, no matter how forgiving and understanding all her family and significant other persons might be. She was unconsciously accepting the brutalities of her husband as a kind of God-given punishment. Because her marriage and her self-esteem were related to her sense of acceptance by God, successful treatment had to grapple with her whole belief system. Her only hope lay in repairing the affirmations of core belief by which she lived, strengthening her grip on life as good, and applying God's justice equally to herself and others.

Simple physical safety required immediate separation from her present husband. She had viewed her visit to the clinic as an effort to gain the strength to tolerate more easily the mistreatment she was receiving. However, the therapist intervened by alerting her parents and family to her dangerous situation and securing court orders for her safety. Carolyn was given space and time to unwind and begin the healing process.

Early treatment focused on reversing her fierce judgments against herself and bringing her self-appraisal more into line with the acceptance God was giving her all along. The therapist told her the story of the woman at the well (John 4), who had married five times (not merely two) and was now cohabiting with still another man. Yet this woman was used by God as the honored first evangelist of the Christian church; after meeting Jesus she had returned to town to cry out, "Come, see a man. . . ." Despite her sins she was given a place in history and used gloriously (or "respectably," in Carolyn's view). God's justice was best served by rehabilitation, not destruction, of even the worst offenders. Its impartial application left lots of room for Carolyn to be accepted by God and employed for great ends.

The key scripture passage for her memorization and frequent recall was 1 John 1:8–9, which reads "If we say that we have no sin, we deceive ourselves, and the truth is not in us. If we confess our sins, he is faithful and just to forgive us our sins, and to cleanse us from all unrighteousness." The meaning of the passage was very clear. The only way Carolyn could avoid being graciously forgiven was to imagine that her laughable little sins were worse than anybody else's. This just was not possible; she had no exclusive rights to any of her failings. God had been forgiving mistakes like hers (and much worse) for centuries—even millennia. God wanted to treat her better than she was treating herself.

Carolyn's recovery was relatively rapid. She saw how terribly she had distorted God's goodness, justice, and impartiality. The therapist then helped her develop a program to plant at deeper levels what she could now understand so rationally. She listened repeatedly to a tape of the story in John 4, and she focused her prayer and devotional life around 1 John 1:8–9 and similar passages. In this way she could break bad emotional and spiritual habits as completely as she had corrected her conscious understandings.

In three months she was liberated and sparkling. Her new job and lighter personal load released marvelous potential that had long been hidden. Her earlier years of hard study and unselfish work for justice were not lost after all. They were like the seed planted that determines the harvest. It was "due season" (Gal. 6:9), and she had finally begun to reap. As Blacks in the ghetto say, "What went around came around." Disbelief was no longer allowed to frustrate God's justice.

Case 5

Burt, age twenty-nine, was an easy mark for the psychological cruelties of the strange family into which he had been born. It never occurred to him that a just God did not want him to define his personal worth by their treatment. He carried their scars for years after leaving his last home among relatives.

A rather promising graduate student, Burt was plagued by periods of deep depression. His studies suffered at these times, but not enough to make him lose his academic standing. He could still move mechanically through many of his assignments. The seriousness of his case stemmed from the awful pain and gloom—the feeling that he had been crying for days at a time. He finally decided to visit the clinic on the advice of a staffer at the agency where he did his field work. He told himself it was more to please this professional than out of any sense that psychiatric help was either possible or deserved.

Analysis revealed that Burt had been an unwanted child, born to a young unwed mother. The love of the grandmother who raised him had been bestowed in fits and starts, since she had serious emotional disturbances of her own. The entire extended family, with whom he had lived at various times and places across the country, tended to reject him. The reasons were both unrelated and obviously related to the circumstances of his birth. Preoccupied with their own struggle, they just never seemed capable of accepting him. His inexplicable academic achievements alienated them from him even more.

Burt's depressions resulted from the usual cause: he had believed their low assessment of him at the deep levels where his moods originated. He was rational enough to know that he was a better-than-average graduate student, but his low self-esteem had been fixed long before his lengthy but successful struggle through college. "I feel like a pure nobody," he said with an almost tearful whimper.

Treatment started with helping Burt to understand his situation. He needed to see that other family members were the really sick ones. He also needed to deal with the marvel of his capabilities in theological terms. Burt had felt that even God was blaming him for his unconventional start in life. His therapist instead reminded him that his intelligence was a special blessing from God. The justice and Providence of God had arranged a compensatory resource that far more than offset his supposed disgrace at birth. Burt sheepishly conceded that he had been too busy looking at what he thought he did not have, to be glad about the most precious of gifts, the talent that he did have.

Next they worked on his deep self-hatred. Burt's agency colleagues were enlisted to give more than usual emphasis to his typically good performance evaluations. At first this made him uncomfortable, because he had been adjusted for so long to a lower self-estimate. With practice he learned to bear the pain of praise, and his core beliefs began to reflect the influence. He listened repeatedly to the Joseph story in Genesis 50, which strengthened his trust in the justice of God. Joseph's older brothers seemed to get away with cruelty, but eventually they had to reap what they had sowed and face their brother in fear and utter dependence.

Another Bible passage helped heal Burt's feelings about his family. Ezekiel the prophet challenged the deep impression that God's justice blames children for their parents' sins. "As the soul of the father is mine, so also is the soul of the son. And the soul that does the sinning, that's the one that's going to die for it" (18:2–4). Repeated hearings began to correct Burt's erroneous feelings about the justice of God.

In the third phase of therapy Burt was assigned to a "family" of surrogate parents. This older couple had lost their son and now were willing to engage in the spiritual parenting of this promising twenty-nine-year-old. Things went well until, unfortunately, Burt's schooling ended and he was relocated. The ties had not developed deeply enough to bear the distance, and Burt's letters and phone calls to his "parents" slowly diminished and finally stopped altogether. He had not completely outgrown his depressions, but he had clearly improved. His firmer grip on the doctrine of divine justice had exploded his devastating core conviction that he was the victim of a depressingly unfair deal from God at birth.

Case 6

Bonnie's case did not take place in the clinics; her help came at a revival. She was not a member of this church; she had come simply because of a warm invitation from a friend. The theme that week was "That Old-Time Religion," and every night the sermon and service were about some affirmation of faith through which older generations of the faithful had coped with the worst of troubles. Bonnie came the night the service was about the justice of God.

The sermon described how ancestors under oppression were surprisingly happy and characterized by goodwill. This was not because they did not know they were being brutalized; they simply saw something most people now do not always see: the justice of God. The preacher chose a text in Galatians on reaping and sowing, emphasizing that evil and evildoers can never triumph ultimately, no matter what seems to be happening now.

The preacher closed with two stories. The first was the slave narrative quoted earlier, in which an exslave in ripe old age rejoiced in the knowledge that ol' Solomon, the boss who tried to stop their prayers, was "burnin' in hell." The story assigned meaning to Bonnie's darkest hours much more than it provided mere delight in divine revenge.

Then the preacher told the story of his son, who had died at age twenty-six from exposure to radiation from atomic physics research. The preacher told of taking comfort from the words of Black songwriter Charles Tindley's gospel hymn, which was then sung in the service:

Trials dark on every hand, and we cannot understand
All the ways that God would lead us
To that blessed Promised Land:
But He guides us with His eye,
And we'll follow 'till we die,
For we'll understand it better by and by.

Bonnie was in her early forties and she had a son in college, so she identified with the speaker. As she sang, her throat choked shut with a big lump. The message of sermon and song somehow struck home, and suddenly she sensed an illuminating insight. If the preacher could wait until later to see God's justice, even for so great a loss as his son's death, could she also trust God's justice for her problem? The service was about to close when Bonnie found herself standing on her feet at the rear of the congregation, and she was talking—testifying!—something she had never done before. Her statement went something like this:

I hope you won't think me rude, but I just *had* to say something. When I came here tonight I was on the verge of a nervous breakdown because of what's been happening to me on my job. I work in the State Office, and I'm the only Black secretary there. The way they harass me keeps me upset all the time. Yet even the ones who treat me nice won't help me by testifying at a hearing. Some of those folks are bent on making me resign or driving me crazy, and I felt so mad and helpless they had almost succeeded. But I want you to know that's all behind me now; they'll never get to me that way again. I've always known there was no way to fight back, and that's what was so frustrating. But now I don't *need* to; while I watch their strange maneuvers, God is watching too. And they're going to reap just what they sow. I feel like a new person. I just want to thank God!

Her eyes filled with tears and she sat down, while a previously hushed audience burst forth with hearty amens. This same doctrinal nourishment had daily kept them whole under such unlikely circumstances. Now Bonnie could join that band of believers. Her change of attitude was not the only goal of the justice of God. The will of God would demand a change in the evil system, but Bonnie's new faith would sustain her until she could join others in bringing about the needed reforms.

The three cases clearly establish the need for rethinking and refining the folk understandings of the justice of God. Popular misconceptions in the imagery of hellfire and damnation rob persons of the healing knowledge that God guarantees meaning to all life by means of just and self-selected recompense. The justice of God, therefore, is good news, not striking terror but conferring hope on captive existence and meaning on all struggles for good. The need for this healing communication of biblical doctrine knows no cultural or ethnic bounds.

4. The Majesty and Omnipotence of God

"Hallelujah: for the Lord God omnipotent reigneth!" (Rev. 19:6)

A third essential core belief undergirding Soul folk has to do with the majesty and Omnipotence of God. If indeed God be God, there can be no outer limit to divine power and no entity capable of opposing it. Nothing can exist that is free of the ultimate control of the Creator and Lord of the universe. Human freedom, of course, amounts to a kind of exception, but it is ordained by God and constitutes a divine self-limitation. Omnipotence means all-powerful; if any strength were capable of resisting the direct edict of the Creator, that strength would itself be the real God. Life is good and Providence is certain, because there can be no ultimately contrary influence.

Omnipotence is essential to the divine guarantee of the goodness and meaningfulness of life. Without it God could not squeeze blessings out of the abuses of human freedom that so often hurt believers. Omnipotence is an abstract term, but it represents God's concrete action in living history. An all-powerful God holds back the Red Sea and implements the divine plan of exodus and liberation. No benevolent plan or kindly attribute of God is worth the mention if God does not have the power to do whatever is involved in making it happen in the real world.

At the same time, Omnipotence is never to be worshiped in isolation or seen as raw power, an end in itself. It is the facilitator of the goodness of God and translates that goodness into the quality of life. This is no Thor, god of thunder, esteemed for the awesomeness of his lightning bolts. Such power without love is tyranny and terror and death. But on the other hand, love without such power is shallow sentimentalism. Life can be worth living only if there is power available to keep it so.

In the modern American culture characterized by a craze for power, the need for core belief about ultimate power is relevant and necessary. The advances of science have freed humanity from the fears once associated with the power of the natural elements. But the movement of humankind into ever larger masses of population and more and more technology has only transferred human helplessness from unpredictable weather to an unmanageable sprawl of modern problems. All people need to know at the core of their being that God's hand holds the whole world.

In Black culture a timeless and universal core belief in the Omnipotence of God surfaces in a variety of ways. Awestruck at the infinitude of the power of God, Soul sisters and brothers rejoiced also that it was on the side of right and righteousness. This awe is documented in the lyrics of spirituals mentioning natural phenomena: "My Lord he calls me, he calls me by the thunder; . . . the lightning. . . . Green trees are bending, poor sinners stand a-trembling; the trumpet sounds withina my soul." Again, the slaves were awed by the fact that "the sun refused to shine" at the Crucifixion, and their response was: "Sometimes it causes me to tremble, tremble, tremble. Were you there. . . ?"

This was, of course, no mere exercise in animistic fear. These same people sang in ethically oriented awe, "My God is so high, you can't git over him; He's so low, you can't git under him; He's so wide, you can't git around him." God guaranteed for them that "Trouble don't last always." In other words, in all of life's experiences, evil's limits were set, and all earth's tyrants were put in their places. They sang it exultantly: "Ride on, King Jesus, no man can hinder thee!"

Outside the Black world, perhaps the best known of all the spirituals says, "He's got the whole world in his hands." It was made famous when the great contralto Marian Anderson sang it to 100,000 people gathered for her concert at the Lincoln Memorial Monument in the nation's capital. The reservations for her concert at the DAR Hall had been cancelled for unjust reasons, and this spiritual affirmed everything that needed to be said in response.

The theological tradition established in the spirituals continues in gospel songs with Omnipotence applied more personally in phrases like these: "The Lord will make a way somehow"; "He opens doors for me, doors I cannot see"; or "Jesus, build a fence all around me." One gospel song establishes the dominant theme: "He is able," and still another declares, "God can do anything but fail."

The Black gospel hymn writer Charles Tindley wrote a moving favorite, "Beams of Heaven," which includes this affirmation: "There is a God that rules above, with hand of power and heart of love, If I am right, He'll fight my battle, I shall have peace some day."

In the hymn tradition that crosses all cultural lines, Black favorites show the same inclination to Omnipotence. The most popular hymns today contain recurring phrases like, "Leaning on the everlasting arms," and "Twas grace that brought me safe thus far." A dramatic favorite alludes to Jesus' calming of the sea and declares, "They all shall sweetly obey thy will. Peace! Be still!" A relative newcomer to the Black repertoire, also adopted directly from White evangelical hymnody and written by Carl Boberg, movingly declares:

Oh Lord, my God, when I in awesome wonder
Consider all the worlds thy hands have made. . . .
Then sings my soul, my Savior God, to thee;
How great thou art, how great thou art!

Hymns both establish and reflect the theology of the singers, and the Omnipotence of God is surely important to Soul folk when judged on these grounds.

With Omnipotence so well established in the musical repertoire of folk worship, it is not surprising that it is reflected in folk prayers and in street sayings. Fluently poetic deacons and sisters call on the Omnipotent Creator with phrases like, "Thou who hast hung the stars in space"; or "Thou who hast scooped out the valleys with thine almighty hand"; or "O Lord, who speakest and the very waves obey. . . ." Later on in a prayer, one can hear, "I know you delivered Daniel in the lions' den"; or, "You heard the three Hebrew children in the fiery furnace"; or, "You answered Paul and Silas when they were in jail, and I know you'll answer your humble servant's prayer." Creative variations on the theme of Omnipotence abound, and they express a widespread cultural fascination of powerless people with a powerful God.

Outside the circles of organized Black religion, the idea is found in abundance, and with varying degrees of seriousness. The exclamation, "Good God A'mighty!" may be heard almost anywhere, regardless of culture, both in the church and on the street. The difference between the church and street is that the Lord's name is used with less inhibition on the streets. People swear by God Almighty, call on the same name in games of cards or craps, and generally manifest the visible amenities of respect for the Deity out of all proportion to their obedience. They have inherited a cultural bias toward belief in God's ability to punish, and they want no part of blatant disrespect, no matter what their lack of commitment to the ways of Christ.

At the heart of all Christian belief is the conviction that the purposes of divine power are unalterably humane and benevolent. Biblical faith holds that, unlike primitive notions about violence and vengeance, the power of God is on the side of love and grace and justice, and above all, Providence. Such a concept of God as power is, even now, almost beyond imagination. The idea of unspeakable power could strike terror, but it is a major part of the good news of the gospel that this power is kindly disposed. It seems too good to be true; God, as seen in Christ, wills abundant life for all who will accept it in faith and commitment. And God has the power to back up the purpose.

The Bible is generously sprinkled with quotations suggesting this Omnipotence. Early in Genesis a question is put to Sarah in her advanced age that is still relevant today: "Is anything too hard for the Lord?" The praise name or title Almighty appears well over fifty times in the Bible, nine of them in the New Testament. One of the most popular verses to employ this title for God is found in the Psalms: "He that dwelleth in the secret places of the most High shall abide under the shadow of the Almighty" (Ps. 91:1). In a still shaky world, one needs the protection of God's Omnipotence.

The doctrine of Omnipotence is a two-edged sword. On the one hand, it is the comfort of all who are oppressed or handicapped. It guarantees that God's love and grace and justice will prevail ultimately in the real world. On the other hand, this same Omnipotence stands over against the injustice, egomania, and self-worship of people like Adolph Hitler. It comforts the afflicted and afflicts the comfortable.

At the very root of the Judeo-Christian tradition is the Exodus, a manifestation of God's Omnipotence, exercised in both roles: liberation for the oppressed and limits for the unjust. Scholars have discovered that it was only after God had delivered the Hebrews that they began to see themselves as a peculiar people, identified with a peculiar faith. Genesis was first written after the power of God had been revealed in the cause of justice at the Red Sea. It was out of this experience of salvation history that they evolved their unique and vitally spiritual breakthrough, the teaching of ethical monotheism. The Shema, or call to worship God as one God, was learned in the experience of the Red Sea. The awesome power revealed there established Jehovah above all local spirits, and deliverance revealed the righteousness and justice of God. Christians, and indeed all persons, still have to know that there is no other God before they can worship and give themselves unreservedly into Jehovah's care. Such a commitment would be meaningless if any other power were able ultimately to frustrate a less than all-powerful God.

This affirmation raises the question of how much freedom we

have in the face of such power. In classical terms, as mentioned at the outset, human freedom is understood as the self-limitation of God. The All-Powerful sets certain limits on the exercise of our power, but God limits God also. If persons are to be free and morally accountable, not just puppets or robots, then God must choose to restrain the power that could have stopped such a cruel act as the Crucifixion. That is how much freedom Omnipotence gives humanity.

Faith in God's power as well as God's self-limitation is seen in the gospel song that declares "God can do anything but fail." This healthy folk belief recognizes also that God as the all-powerful could never cease to be. The eternal God is powerful enough to exercise self-restraint.

The final answer to problems of fitting together justice and Omnipotence, Providence and omniscience is that God has a plan. It leaves room for the evil exercise of individual freedom, but it sets limits beyond which that freedom may not go (Job 1:10–12). Hitler came close to ruling our world, but there was a limit set on his power. History shows the awesome exercise of Omnipotence in bringing his forces to an unpredictable halt.

God works in everything and always has a contingent plan by which to wring out a blessing. God's knowledge and power are self-limited only to make room for our choice and the exercise of that choice. For Joseph who was falsely imprisoned, God had a plan by which to elevate him to prime minister (Gen. 50:20). The whole challenge of qualified or restricted Omnipotence is answered at the higher level of God's plan or purpose, and the elevation of Joseph to the prime ministership is in many ways at least as awesome as the opening of the Red Sea.

Thus, the goodness of God and of life is celebrated in the certainty that all these hard trials fit into a higher plan that guarantees meaning in life, opposing absurdity, and keeping life worth living. That plan is being implemented by all necessary power, and the angels in heaven sing, "Hallelujah, for the Lord God Omnipotent reigneth" (Rev. 19:6). Healthy, whole existence in the world today demands that we join the angels, no matter what our race or class. The song must come from our very depths—from the level of core belief.

The cases of Eva, Barbara, and Rick illustrate how crucial this core belief can be.

Case 7

Eva needed to know God's power above all powers and God's good above all goods, even above the male friend she idolized. At twenty-eight, after her third suicide attempt, she had been referred by her physician for counseling. Thus, the primary purpose of her visit was to manage the crisis of her desire to die.

She was depressed and heavily dependent on sedatives. Her last suicide attempt, like the others, came when her boyfriend, whom she had met at work, threatened to break away from her and return to his legal wife. He, much more than her previous lovers, had really helped her and brightened up her life. If he were to break off their relationship, even though she agreed that it was right for him to be a better husband, she felt she might as well be dead. She also stated, "He means more to me than life itself. I would fall on my knees before him if he told me to." The strange twist in this devotion was that she called a professional, not her boyfriend, after she had overdosed, and she thus participated in saving her own life.

Eva had been a neglected middle child in a large family, with a father who loved her "deeply" when sober, which was rarely. He was detached and uncaring most of the time, a fact she knew but was reluctant to face. Her mother was a dull, passive woman of no apparent significance to her daughter. Eva lived a very uneventful life and was a fully undistinguished high school student and family member. She was so invisible that she had had to raise herself.

As she grew older and left home, the load of being without assistance and emotional support weighed heavier and heavier. Twice she found lovers who met some of her needs while exploiting her, but in each case her severe emotional dependence overtaxed their commitment, and they withdrew. Both times Eva was shattered and tried to commit suicide. After each, her physician put her on tranquilizers, and she developed an increasing dependence on drugs. The depression thus treated was never helped; her sense of being a nobody only increased.

In the emergency treatment given, she was helped to face the limitations of her boyfriend and challenged to choose between him and the God of unlimited power. She was further led to understand that her angry attitude toward the real authorities and powers of this life was self-defeating. She had been created by God, in whose sight she was of far more worth than she could face comfortably. The power to kill herself was not unusual, while God's power to give life was truly awesome. How would she face her Maker after death, if she had committed suicide just to escape pain and distress? The therapist gained some leverage from Eva's personal belief system, since she saw herself as quite religious. He prescribed that she read Matt. 10:28 daily, reminding her that it is foolish to fear mere men, or the loss of them. If one must temporarily fear, the One to fear is God who is able to destroy both body and soul.

On the positive side, Eva engaged in disciplines of exercise, prayer, and meditation. The therapist suggested a passage from 2 Cor. to chip away at her sense of being a nobody. The Apostle Paul asks God to take away his "thorn in the flesh"—his weakness or flaw—and God replies that divine grace is sufficient (powerful enough) for him, because human strength is made perfect in weakness (2 Cor. 12:9). The believer's limited strength is supplemented by God's power.

Eva was therefore not required to continue developing on her own all the resources she needed. She could lean on God's powers when hers ran out, a normal response that even Paul, the genius of the early church, had found necessary. Like him, she too was a person of worth and power in God's sight. She had permission to be happy and to be fulfilled.

Eva's therapy was classified as emergency and was therefore

terminated after only twelve sessions, when she no longer considered suicide a real option. By that time her depression had decreased, and she was much more happily relating to the God about whom she had known without proper awareness and feelings. She could safely transfer her dependency to the One who could be depended on to be unchangeably loving and able to provide for her in all real needs. The therapist helped her find a network in which this core belief was lived out, and he advised her to continue treatment.

Case 8

Barbara's manipulative mother was the real power and authority in her life. She needed a deliverer to overcome her carefully planned and executed entrapment.

Barbara, age thirty-one, sought help for a weight problem. However, when the therapist asked about her emotional health, it became immediately clear that she had chosen the clinic over a weight-loss program because of an intuition that she needed further help. She answered most cooperatively, even happily, and the conversation never returned to the subject of weight in the entire brief course of therapy.

Barbara lived with her eleven-year-old daughter and her mother. She was plagued by obsessive thoughts and compulsive behavior, and she was therefore very shy and pessimistic about relating to anyone outside a narrow circle of familiar associates.

She had had a happy early childhood with her father, but he had been yanked out of her life at age five when her parents divorced. Her mother had then set out to displace him completely, discrediting him maliciously and contriving to make Barbara solely dependent on her. This made Barbara a readily available target for the anger her mother could not vent on her exhusband. Her mother discouraged any attempt on Barbara's part to grow up and live a life of her own.

Barbara's problems multiplied when she bore a child before

the age of twenty in a very brief attempt to escape her mother's dominance. She became all the more inadequate and dependent, and she dared not express the deep anger she felt towards her mother, since she received from her much-needed shelter and child care. Her curious love/hate for her mother was further complicated by utter awe of her power. Barbara attended church, but this influence did little to lower her dread of her mother, since she had been taught that God's power, like her mother's, was used exclusively to punish.

Sensing that therapy was the key to her deliverance, Barbara took the tests and followed the instructions well. When she and the therapist had identified what she really wanted to do in life, they moved on to the obstacle keeping her from fulfilling her goals—her mother's dominance. They faced her mother's feet of clay and the fact that the power used by this tyrant was not hers but God's, available to all, including Barbara. Barbara learned to recognize that she already owned this power; through her job she paid bills and spared her mother the rigors of a regular job. This helped to break the spell of dominance, and the mother grudgingly settled for Barbara's becoming much more her own woman.

Specific treatment included listening regularly to Bible passages like Paul's account of weakness in 2 Corinthians. This helped her in her weakness to live from the power of the Almighty. She viewed her church activities in a new light, and she grew rapidly both emotionally and spiritually. When her eight sessions were completed, she had identified and relinquished many of her real problems. She was now confident in her own gifts and open to the Omnipotent God.

Case 9

Rick thought that he himself was omnipotent, and that perhaps he could even stand up against God. When inquiring by phone about the therapists at the clinic he made it clear that he demanded real service from them.

Rick was twenty-one and had been in a wheelchair for two years as a result of an auto accident. The original diagnosis of severed spine had been changed to compressed spine, so there was some hope that he might regain the use of his legs. He talked matter-of-factly about his reckless years, and he mentioned that his girlfriend had died in the accident that had paralyzed him. He was trying to find a reason for living after these disasters.

Rick had been a difficult child. His parents, overjoyed at the birth of their only child, had failed to discipline him properly. His mother had catered to his every whim, while his father had avoided confronting him except in dire emergencies. He had been sent home from kindergarten four or five times because his teacher found him uncontrollable. While he was known to have potential, he had never used it and had been considered a terror all the way through school. He was insensitive to his own or anyone else's needs, and when his parents gave him a car at age sixteen, he had two accidents in two years. Since only the cars had been damaged, Rick's reckless habits were not curbed.

At nineteen he was out driving fast with his girlfriend. Pam asked him to slow down, but it was too late. When the dust settled, he was paralyzed from the hips down, and she was pronounced dead.

At first, Rick showed no feelings when he mentioned Pam's death, and he become irritated when the therapist probed his reactions. He was accustomed to having things on his own terms, and did not want to talk about her death. In the seventh session, after all the case history and relaxation and prayer, the therapist moved into the forbidden territory. He asked Rick to commit himself to God rather than to continue to speak as if God were as manipulable as his parents. God had the power to do all the things Rick wanted and needed to do, but not on Rick's terms. If he would surrender his recklessness, about which he bragged in covert but revealing ways, God was willing to forgive and to heal, and God had the power to do it.

The next session the therapist opened an even touchier topic, whether or not Rick really wanted to walk again. At this, Rick exploded. The therapist still calmly insisted that God would help him to walk and would forgive him for killing Pam, the major issue that had been carefully avoided up to that point. Rick became hysterical, rose up from the therapist's chair, and *walked* twelve feet back to his wheelchair. As he roared out of the office, he shouted that he would never return. He also paused long enough to declare, "It was your all-powerful God who punished me with paralysis and who took my girlfriend! Why doesn't he bring her back?"

Obviously, this case was not cured in the professional sense. Rick left therapy before his problem had been resolved. But he did walk for the first time in two years. He also uncovered his real problem, a bodacious attempt to manipulate Almighty God in the same way he had controlled his parents all these years. The therapist could only hope that he would soon wake up and see for himself the facts now so clearly evident from his behavior.

A proper understanding of the Omnipotence of God could have saved Rick, Eva, and Barbara a lot of mistakes and personality disorders. One either knows God the Omnipotent or risks being one's own omnipotence, fostering either a sense of utter inadequacy or a dangerous break with reality.

5. The Omniscience of God

"Your Father knoweth what things ye have need of, before ye ask."
(Matt. 6:8)

The omniscience of God is another core belief that implements and perfects Providence while undergirding the goodness of life for Soul folk. This doctrine affirms that God knows everything. The God of Providence and Omnipotence is neither without the power to determine that life shall be good, nor the wisdom to detect what that good should be. Furthermore, divine justice would not be worthwhile if it were really blind. The blindfold on the figure symbolizing justice is designed to show impartiality only. The virtually worldwide symbol for the all-knowingness of God, across cultural as well as religious lines, is an open, penetrating eye. All sorts of people refer to divine omniscience in all sorts of situations; without a moment's hesitation, they will say, "God knows."

If life is to be meaningful and satisfying, God must be all-knowing. To be sure, justice is indispensable, but equity would be severely limited without omniscience. God, simply to be God, must supersede all other intelligence, but that same Deity must also know human limits in order to implement the intent that life shall be abundant. In addition, the Lord of the universe must know when and how to exercise Omnipotence to relieve stressful situations and keep life within bearable bounds. Such are the many implications of the doctrine, yet all this is seldom formally mentioned, even though it is constantly implied in casual conversations amidst the stresses of life.

Black culture has always included this doctrine among its core beliefs. Without ever using such terms as omniscience, the basic belief system of Soul folk includes the certainty that God knows all. This affirmation did not appear from nowhere when Blacks came to these shores; it developed out of their prior African traditional religion. Numberless proverbs declare it, and it is deeply imbedded in the psyche of all children reared in the typical cultures of the sub-Sahara. A Yoruba proverb says, "Olorun nikan l' o qbon"; or, "The uncreated High God of Heaven [head of a monotheistic bureaucracy] alone is wise." Among the many praise names for God (actually a folk corpus of working theology) is the Ashanti's "Brekyirihunuade." It means, "He who knows or sees all, before and behind, the omniscient." Traditional Africans shared abundant sayings about the inability to hide things from God, all suggesting an omniscience that guarantees both the justice and the meaningfulness that make life abundantly good.

The slaves' spiritual genius for seeing God and life as good despite their unmerited sufferings was built on the same folk sayings and wisdom. They sang, "There's no hiding place down here. . . . I ran to the rock, to hide my face; the rock cried out no hiding place! There's no hiding place down here." Or, again, "My God is writin' all the time. . . . He sees all you do, an' he hears all you say. My God is writin' all the time." Here one notices that their notions of omniscience included the use of the ear figure as well as the eyes. They also sang, "King Jesus is a'list'nin' all night long . . . to hear some sinner pray." There is a certain sophistication evident in this ability to see omniscience as judgment and comfort at the same time.

Modern gospel songs, born in America's depression of the 1930s, placed more emphasis on God's ability to comfort. The idea that God knows "just how much we can bear," implied in the stories at the very beginning of the first chapter, comes from a song of this vintage. Roberta Martin's song of this title was and is tremendously influential in promulgating the folk doctrine that God keeps even the woes of a depression within human tolerance. Another very popular gospel song of the same era was Lucie Campbell's paean of praise to God's omniscience:

If when you give the best of your service,
Telling the world that the Savior is come;
Be not dismayed when men won't believe you;
He understands; He'll say, "Well done."

God's unlimited access to truth is here more than impressive, abstract wisdom. God is the all-wise protector from too much trouble and the warm understander of the unjustly accused and painfully misunderstood.

Popular hymns from the repertoire of hymns common to both Black and White cultures equally emphasize omniscience. One of the two or three most widely sung hymns is, "What a Friend We Have in Jesus." It includes:

Have we trials and temptations?
Is there trouble anywhere?
Jesus knows our every weakness;
Take it to the Lord in prayer.

The chorus of the popular "No, Not One!" declares, "Jesus knows all about our struggles, He will guide till the day is done." This theme of divine guidance strongly implies omniscience, and it is found in numberless hymns used constantly in the Black church. "Guide Me, O Thou Great Jehovah" and "All the Way My Savior Leads Me" are but two of a vast collection of such hymns of assurance. The strength of this great affirmation among Blacks is no mystery when one considers their hymnody.

The word "omniscience" is seldom used in folk conversation, but the words of ordinary people in both street and church abound in references to it. Here are typical scenarios. A careful driver has just hit a three-year-old child who darted suddenly into the street after a ball. He tells the distraught mother, "God knows I did my best to stop." Again, a husband accuses his wife of dancing too often with his single friend. Her unconsciously theological reply is common: "God knows my heart." When a child buttresses a report with, "Cross my heart and hope to die," she or he implies the same appeal to omniscience.

This folk resort to the omniscience of God knows few cultural or ethnic limits.

Appeal to God's omniscience is no recent or novel development; the human condition has required theological resources such as this from early in its history. The writers of the Psalms took comfort from God's omniscience. One said, "He knoweth the secrets of the heart" (44:21), while another confessed, "His understanding is infinite" (147:5). The entire 139th Psalm affirms God's omniscience and omnipresence:

O Lord, Thou hast searched me, and known me.
Thou knowest my downsitting and mine uprising;
Thou understandest my thought afar off.
Thou compassest my path and my lying down,
And art acquainted with all my ways.
For there is no word in my mouth, but,
Lo, O Lord, thou knowest it altogether.
Thou has beset me behind and before,
And laid thine hand upon me.
Such knowledge is too wonderful for me;
It is high, I cannot attain unto it.

. . . .

For thou hast possessed my reins:
Thou hast covered me in my mother's womb.
I will praise thee;
For I am fearfully and wonderfully made:
Marvelous are thy works;
And that my soul knoweth right well

. . . .

Search me, O God, and know my heart:
Try me, and know my thoughts:
And see if there be any wicked way in me,
And lead me in the way everlasting.

The folk wisdom of the book of Proverbs also witnesses to this doctrine: "The eyes of the Lord are in every place, Beholding the evil and the good" (40:28).

Other writers attest that the assumption is beyond question. Job, the man of many troubles, said, "No thought can be withholden from God" (42:2). The prophet Isaiah declared that there is "no searching of His understanding" (40:28). Paul wrote that God searches human hearts (Rom. 8:27). The book of Hebrews proclaimed, "All things are naked and opened unto God" (4:13). Jesus stated in clearest terms that God's wisdom is humanely focused when he said, "Your Father knoweth what things ye have need of, before ye ask Him" (Matt. 6:8). Mention has already been made of Paul's declaration that our troubles are not unique, and that God will not allow us to be tested beyond our limit, making sure that we are able to bear whatever happens (1 Cor. 10:13). Obviously, God's Providence is trustworthy because of this intimate knowledge of us and of our limitations. As the psalmist put it, "He knoweth our frame; and He remembereth that we are dust" (103:14).

Black slaves accepted biblical affirmations such as these and added them to a foundation of African traditional religion. Together they provided the strong roots out of which came the still pervasive affirmation among Soul folk that God's ultimate wisdom is applied to the warm understanding and care and protection of the faithful.

Although reference to God's omniscience pervades casual conversation, many fail to trust it deeply at the level of core belief. This deficit in faith often goes undetected because it is almost always mixed with absence of belief in other attributes of God, such as Providence or justice. The cases that follow illustrate this characteristic. Carol, Mike, and Cynthia share a tendency to fear that they have reached or are about to reach their limits. It is hard for them to affirm life and hold fast to the belief that God does know how sincerely they are trying and how much they can endure. They imply casual belief in omniscience, but they feel that God is demanding too much or letting life demand too much of them.

Case 10

Carol, age thirty-seven, visited the therapist because her life was frenzied. Thoughts raced through her mind erratically and at high speeds. Her pattern of activities was disorganized and overcrowded. Tired and yet unable to sleep, she seemed irresistibly drawn into more and more obligations. She was diagnosed as being in the manic stage of a manic-depressive disorder, now called a bipolar personality.

After a complete physical exam Carol was placed on a strict diet and ordered off all refined sugars. Her psychological profile revealed that she had been born by breech birth, a painful struggle that her mother referred to often to keep Carol manipulable. Thus Carol's vision of life was that of a perpetual struggle, with survival itself constantly at stake. She had been made to feel ashamed of her birth, and she often wished she had never been born. The pressure had increased when at age seven she was ordered by her grandmother to be a success and never to depend on anyone except herself. Pressure to be self-sufficient increased three years later when her father abandoned them and her mother went to work. The next year her grandmother died, forcing her into further responsibility. At age twenty, Carol had become a nurse in order to serve people. At twenty-one she married and took on the role of helping her husband. Motherhood followed at age twenty-two, and Carol's load now included a young child. Responsibility escalated from there until, at age thirty-seven, Carol was over her head in helping activities, at home, at church, and in her community.

In treatment, Carol's rigid drive was unmasked as an overdose of socialization. In other words, she had heard too many demands from parent figures, and she had taken them too uncritically and much too seriously. Carol's life had been further complicated by "secondary gains," hidden advantages she had received from her unhealthy habits. She felt power and control over the people helped, and she reinforced her vision of life as an inevitable struggle. Even more deeply, Carol's overload of commitments confirmed her mother's implied judgment that she was a failure and should never have been born.

Carol learned to relax and to accept release from all the demands that had been laid on her, not by God, but by relatives and groups. A shift to the other pole of deep depression was averted by helping her tone down her ambitions, prune her involvements without embarrassment, and accept herself at the level of performance to which an all-knowing God had assigned her. The hardest demands to let go were those from the departed grandmother, but eventually Carol replaced her too by the much more knowledgeable Lord.

Carol is now living a relatively active life, utilizing her good health and high energy levels, but she has accepted divine approval for a program within her reach. This did not happen overnight; it took thirty-two sessions over a period of more than eight months. But she is doing well, trusting God to know what should be expected of her even when others do not.

Case 11

When Mike, age thirty-four, wandered into the office, he said he was there to please his new girlfriend. She was concerned about his casual mention of possibly blowing up his former employer's business. Without admitting any specific problem, Mike went through analysis cooperatively, and the therapist met what turned out to be two totally different people.

Mike played two distinct roles: the adult cold-blooded killer, whose bragging about deadly exploits would send chills down any normal person's spine; and the little child scared to fight, who was pushing the killer to spill out his uneasiness about participating in those atrocities and thereby to register a cry for help. The blood and guts stories were real, since Mike had been trained as a commando and had served with distinction in the war in Vietnam. In fact, the methods of search and destroy and kill were by far his best-developed skills.

Adopted as a baby, Mike had been smaller and less physically developed than his father had hoped he would be. Mike suffered a low self-esteem in the first place because his natural parents had let him be adopted, but parental demands increased his self-doubt. Mike resented the martial arts courses his father demanded, and his peaceful disposition later surrendered only partially to the pressures of military commando training. He became a proficient killer, but he still saw himself as a coward; in Vietnam he had been too frightened to ever sleep soundly.

The little boy in Mike cooperated with the therapist because he was afraid the other Mike might really hurt or kill someone. The anger that could trigger it all grew out of what he saw as a lifelong and utterly unbearable series of injustices. In addition to his parents' failure to communicate love effectively and his unusually high number in the draft lottery, his current girlfriend had sent him a "Dear John" letter, terminating his warmest relationship to that date. After the war, no one in the States had cared much what happened to him. Veteran status helped very little, and he moved from one poor job to another. Aside from the blessing of the new romantic attachment that had caused him to see the therapist, Mike saw all of his experience as hostile, aided by his own increasing hostility that invited further indignities. His ultimate question was, "Good or bad or indifferent, how is anybody supposed to be able to take all this?"

Mike accepted the methodical disciplines of his treatment, because he had become used to military regulations. Psychomechanics and biofeedback appealed to him, and he was helped to express his anger in nonthreatening ways. He secured a marvelously appropriate part-time job teaching martial arts in addition to a regular job in physically exhausting labor. He was helped to see that God had not directly willed the abuses heaped on him, and God had in fact set a limit for them. Furthermore, the teaching job was just the beginning of God's plan to squeeze blessings out of the worst things that freedom allowed others to do to him. Mike soon qualified for a loan and bought the first new car of his life, which relieved his anger and frustration still more. For his own sanity and wholeness, he was taught to forgive the uncaring world and to appreciate the parents who did care for him in their own way throughout his childhood.

As Mike left therapy, he gave thanks for his new opportunities that opened up just in time. The omniscient One had known just when to halt the disasters and provide relief. It never occurred to him that part of his new peace came when he began to unwind and to treat people with warmth and relaxed sensitivity.

Case 12

Cynthia's physician referred her because she thought she was going to die and had symptoms to prove it: shortness of breath, chest pains, and feelings of faintness. She felt unloved and became angry when her husband, children, or parents refused her impulsive demands. She would suffer fits of pain and panic when her husband wanted to be intimately affectionate. Sighing deeply, Cynthia exclaimed that she was near the end of her endurance.

Her detailed case history was quite revealing. She saw her early childhood as idyllic, since she had been allowed to do pretty much as she pleased. Then, when she was nine, the family's finances plummeted, and they had to move to a much less comfortable setting. All her fun came to a screeching halt, and "it was never the same after that." She made two revealing statements: "I still hate surprises like moving," and, "Sometimes I feel like I'm still nine years old."

Her illnesses were further complicated by a heavy sense of guilt. The first enjoyment she had experienced after the age of nine came from an uncle who played with her in ways that were sexually inappropriate. Since she had liked it, she came to feel that she was basically "naughty." A brief extramarital affair after the birth of her children had only added to the fear that her wickedness might get out of hand. To deny her guilt and avoid other adult responses and responsibilities, she retained childish responses to stressful situations. When tantrums failed to solve them, she was seized by a formless, free-floating fear—an overwhelming panic and terror. She had been unable to mature emotionally beyond the age of nine.

Cynthia's immediate treatment dealt with controlling the symptoms of her illness by gaining control of her galloping panic. She identified issues that triggered spells of panic and sickness. She was then taught disciplines of relaxation to use when the symptoms first appeared,

Her longterm treatment involved working with her belief system. Cynthia slowly replaced her ideal vision of childhood with a picture of a safe and happy and productive adulthood. This new dream was planted by first gaining her thoughtful agreement, then by providing tapes that strongly affirmed the opposites of her fears. This partially devotional exercise included assurances of God's love and protection. Her certainty that nobody knew her tortures was offset with the deeper conviction that God knows and understands every problem and every one of her limitations. She came to recite repeatedly an affirmation composed for her: "God loves me, protects me, and knows just how much I can bear. So I release my fears completely and rejoice in the abundant life God has willed for me."

With this growing certainty, Cynthia felt she had received permission to grow and progress through the natural stages of maturity up to her current chronological age. She improved in her efforts to nip anxiety attacks in the bud, and she saw herself in much more positive terms. The temper tantrums disappeared, and her impulsive demands sharply decreased, often being withdrawn even after they were made. Her entire family noted her progress and agreed to enter into therapy with her. In seven and a half months, Cynthia had become convinced that God had known just when to intervene and save her from disaster. The future now seemed bright indeed.

As long as so many disturbed and oppressed adults keep thinking they are close to their breaking points, they will continue to need both the affirmation and therapeutic elaboration of the doctrine of the omniscience of God. The belief that God knows and understands provides a basis for coping and is essential to a healthy grasp on reality. Without it, the future is closed and all efforts are in vain. When life is guaranteed to be within manageable bounds and the sincerity of one's efforts is sure to be understood by God, one can survive and be whole, no matter what.

6. The Goodness of God and Creation

"And God saw every thing that He had made, and, behold, it was very good." (Gen. 1:31)

The most pervasive of all the divine attributes included under Providence is the goodness of Creator and creation. Yet the goodness of God has sounded too obvious to justify extended treatment in either spontaneous folk motif or formal theological writings. Also, the word *good* has seemed to convey a vague and innocuous meaning. It becomes more specific, however, if contrasted with its opposite, as a negative rather than positive world view. When a culture holds to the former, all of life is considered a struggle between the self and the environment, which is assumed to be alien and hostile. A negative world view mistrusts nature and all human society. On the other hand, a positive world view is compatible with Providence in the belief that the experience of creation and life itself must be ultimately beneficial or good. In this mood, life is always worth more than death, and this attitude is at the very heart of emotional and spiritual wholeness.

In other words, the certainty of the basic goodness of the earth and of the human sojourn is essential to total well-being. Yet, understandably, Western culture has not uniformly believed this. Subzero winter winds conveyed opposite impressions of the earth to pre-Christian Northern Europeans. Likewise, the desperate competition for the very limited supply of safe caves did little to enhance the prehistoric root view of human nature. Meanwhile, pre-Christian Greek dualism had so influenced the gospel that when it arrived in Europe, its witness about creation and human nature was heavily mixed.

Pauline and Augustinian suspicions of "worldly" things were echoed effectively in Calvinism. So the goodness of life and its Author became at best a muted message. On a culturewide basis, one best reads the results in the corpus of the most popular American hymns. Of the two which follow, the first has had much wider use and deeper impact than the latter:

Amazing grace! how sweet the sound,
That saved a wretch like me!
I once was lost, but now I'm found,
Was blind, but now I see.

(John Newton)

For the beauty of the earth,
For the glory of the skies,
For the love which from our birth
Over and around us lies:
Lord of all, to thee we raise
This our hymn of grateful praise.

(Folliott S. Pierpoint)

Americans in general believe only halfheartedly that a good God is everywhere present in a good creation, which is dwelt in by people made in the divine image. The Soul system echoes this deficit in faith. "Amazing Grace" has been so fully adopted as to become the uncontested favorite hymn of the Black church. With this great hymn and others like it, Protestant theology was more than incidentally impressed upon the minds of slaves. However, the conquest of African and Old Testament positive world views was far from complete. An accurate account of Black folk faith must at the outset treat their dominantly positive beliefs about the Creator and about life in the creation. Had they believed otherwise, they could never have survived the hardships of bondage.

The praise of God and its counterpart, celebration of the goodness of life, are outstanding characteristics of Black religion and indeed Black culture. Blacks have praised God for centuries, throughout the darkest moments of slavery, by celebrating the smallest blessings from God. Their descendents have hardly changed this pattern of celebration and praise.

How, then, did this theme of the goodness of God and life survive the onslaughts of slavery and otherworldly theology? The answer lies in the pattern of inherited culture synthesized with biblical insight already noticed in previous chapters. Here the African traditional and biblical sources will be considered together, along with the related message of Black spirituals.

On the goodness of the universe, African traditional religion spoke with the same voice as the Old Testament. The Ashanti expressed it in a proverb: "The hawk poised aloft says, 'All things that the Supreme Being made are beautiful (or good).'" This is virtually the equivalent of the Genesis statement, "God saw everything that he had made, and, behold it was very good" (1:31). Black slaves had little reason to view the universe positively, but even so they sang things like, "On my journey now. . . . Well I wouldn't take nothin' for my journey now." A certain spiritual genius combined the old-country tradition and the newfound Bible to keep the faith in the goodness of creation, their hardships notwithstanding.

Perhaps the best New Testament statement of this faith is found in Ephesians 4. "God is above all, and through all, and in you all" (v.6). This powerful affirmation includes (1) the presence of God as ruler and regulator of all creation (Omnipotence); (2) the presence of God as mystical personal companion and liberating Holy Spirit (omnipresence); (3) the resulting potential for good, in all of which God so richly dwells, including human beings. This text expresses the belief in an indwelling divine spirit that is so common in African tradition and so often misread as animism. The spirit possession it implies is common to both cultures. In both cases, the universe is holistic, with no division between the sacred and secular realms. A deep affirmation of the message common to both is healing indeed.

However, neither African nor biblical views are naive. Thousands of tribal proverbs recognize the existence of evil and offer sage advice. The most-loved Psalm in the Bible, the twenty-third, combines the awareness of evil enemies with the goodness of God and life:

Yea, though I walk through the valley of the shadow of death,
I will fear no evil: for thou art with me;
Thy rod and thy staff they comfort me.
Thou preparest a table before me in the presence of mine enemies:
Thou anointest my head with oil; my cup runneth over.
Surely goodness and mercy shall follow me all the days of my life:
And I will dwell in the house of the Lord forever (4–6).

The awareness of trouble is, likewise, often apparent in the spirituals, but it is also tempered with such insights as, "I'm so glad trouble don't last always." This philosophical comfort is widely paralleled in African wisdom. The Yoruba advise, "the trouble that causes so much anxiety will be overcome; a red eye is not necessarily blind." Others say, "What storm is there which has no end?" Still another tribe says, "No matter how long the night, the day is sure to come." These sayings parallel the biblical witness in Isaiah: "When thou passest through the waters, I will be with thee; and through the rivers, they shall not overflow thee; when thou walkest through the fire, thou shalt not be burned; neither shall the flame kindle upon thee" (43:2). Here God is recognized as omniscient and Omnipotent, the One who limits troubles and assures life's goodness.

Further, Blacks view human beings as part of God's good creation. Even the worst inhumane treatment never convinced most slaves to accept Calvinist theories of total human depravity. They often sang of sinners, but they never expressed a loss of hope. They expressed their positive view of human nature in their attitude towards children, a view stemming directly from African tradition. The Ashanti and many others declare that nobody has to show God to a child. Each person is considered an offspring of God; none is a child of the earth. Parents just accept custody of children who really belong to God. All this is not far from the Genesis account that declares that humankind is crafted in the very image of God (1:26). So long as that likeness cannot be totally obliterated, the Soul system will always be on sound biblical ground in its celebration of the goodness of God and of human existence in creation.

This positive world view is expressed in numberless examples of gospels and popular hymns. The most explicit of the gospel songs declares, despite all possible appearances to the contrary, "There's a bright side somewhere. . . . Don't you stop until you find it" (James Cleveland). To this can be added the assurance that "The Lord will make a way somehow" (Thomas Dorsey). Another popular gospel song personalizes God's goodness: "God is so good to me. . . . I don't serve him as I should, I don't deserve all of this good; So many things are not as they should be, but God is so good to me" (Doris Akers).

Black hymns, like gospel songs, relate the goodness of life to the care and provision of God. They may sometimes imply that God cares only for the Soul, but even this guarantees a good life. The crucial thing is that one must trust, a major theme in the belief of Blacks.

I trust in God wherever I may be,
Upon the land or on the rolling sea,
For, come what may, from day to day,
My Heavenly Father watches over me.

                                                    (W. C. Martin)

God guarantees goodness throughout all aspects of life. "Earth has no sorrow that heaven cannot heal," proclaims one song. "His eye is on the sparrow, and I know he watches me. I sing because I'm happy," confesses another. This goodness in gospel songs and hymns applies to the individual person as well as to life in general. So Lucie Campbell wrote of the "Something within me that holdeth the reins. . . . Something within me I cannot explain," suggesting a human nobility worth celebrating. This obviously refers also the indwelling of something from beyond, namely the Holy Spirit. Belief in the Spirit's indwelling is the successor to the African tradition of spirit possession.

The ecstatic indwelling of the Holy Spirit in the physical temple of the crying, shouting believer is undoubtedly the most complete affirmation of the worth of that person in the sight of God. This complete acceptance is most manifest among Holiness or Pentecostal groups whose rhetoric about the human body is very negative. However, the negative things that Soul folk sing and say are not always the things they really believe and do. The "something within" that moves them may work more healing than the negative rhetoric can hurt. God uses and accepts all of a human being, in worship as well as in work.

The implications of a holy dance are a powerful antidote for a negative world view and unhealthy dualism. Dance views the whole human frame unashamedly as worthy for praising God. One can use the feet, the head, the elbows, and even the parts that Paul called "uncomely." Further, since the dance is considered the act of the Holy Ghost or Holy Spirit, the very Creator is personally present in the dancer. One cannot escape the implied potential goodness of the "flesh" used to praise God.

The incidence of personality disorder among Soul sisters and brothers is somewhat proportional to the deterioration of the Black belief system. In fact, persons of any background would fare better with a life-celebrating frame of mind such as the one reflected in the spiritual: "Keep so busy praisin' my Jesus, ain't got time to die."

In the three cases that follow, each person lacks an awareness of the elements in every life that are a basis for celebration and praise. Each has missed the reality of the goodness of God, everywhere present in a good creation.

Case 13

Christine, age twenty-six, was referred to the clinic by the latest in her long series of physicians. She had had severe pain in her joints, terrifying heart palpitations, nauseous stomach aches, and spells of weakness so great she could hardly walk or talk. Previously prescribed exercise had been impossible because, as she said, "My body is on strike." She reported it almost as if her body really belonged to somebody else and had a mind of its own. In the classic terms of the dualistic conflict of spirit versus flesh, her flesh was more than usually evil, and what was worse, it was clearly winning the battle.

Born prematurely in hard labor, Christine had been immediately plagued with temperature malfunction and a series of lung problems and pneumonias that had stretched throughout childhood. Because the tender care disappeared as soon as her condition was no longer critical, her earliest memories associated survival with loving care administered in a context of disease. Naturally she continued unconsciously to invent new illnesses to ensure further care.

On a conscious level, Christine felt cheated and defeated by life. She was haunted by the idea that all the earth was joined in a conspiracy against her, a conspiracy plotted originally by her own terrible body. In her eyes, her accusations were sincere and her martyrdom real.

Since her problems were vast, counseling goals were scaled down to something within feasible reach. The physician and the therapist agreed on a limited contract designed to identify and enhance Christine's awareness of the good things manifest in her life and in herself, and then see if the changed outlook would be at all helpful in reducing her symptoms. Her prognosis was "fair to poor."

As Christine learned and used techniques for reducing stress, her medications were reduced. Major diet changes were also employed. Her functioning on the job and in her family was studied in order to evaluate her complaint that others never understood how hard she was trying to please them and to carry her personal responsibilities. She was assigned research to find all the good things she could about herself, her family, and her boss. This helped her begin to see how much she had lived in an infantile fantasy designed to serve her needs only. Deep depression over her foibles was avoided by receiving approval for her sincere effort.

The therapist led Christine through a series of self-affirmations. One of these was the widely known, "Every day, in every way, I am getting better and better," which Christine applied to her health and her growing maturity. God's verdict in Gen. 1:31 that everything created was good was used to chip away at her pessimistic dualism about her physical being. On the basis of this insight, Christine began to engage in limited experiences of actual enjoyment, which led to an expanded vision of the possibilities for a happier and more healthy life.

In a lengthy thirty-six sessions her prognosis moved to simply "fair," but her progress and her enjoyment of her sizeable homework assignments made her determined to continue the process.

Case 14

Perpetual headaches and deep depression motivated Marsha, age thirty-nine, to seek more assistance than her physician could give. Both consciously and unconsciously, she perceived life as unbearable. She could not view suicide as an escape, partly as a result of receiving Roman Catholic teaching early in life, but mostly because of her inquiry into Eastern religions. The idea of the soul's transmigration, or reincarnation, promised only future problems in a coming life. There was no point in postponing the resolution of her problems. She decided to face them squarely here and now.

Life's unbearability had begun as a child when both parents were absent because of work. Her mother was distant even when at home. Her dominant father had wanted this only child to be a boy, and he therefore viewed her ambivalently. Thus Marsha felt an early, pervasive loneliness, and she had long hours in which to regret her gender. The pattern continued in college and a childless marriage. Her husband had been the exact duplicate of her distant father, and he had finally left her two years before, with no explanation. This devastation had brought on the deep depressions and chronic headaches. She could keep her job only because it required no human response or growth, and the only assistance it offered was financial.

No therapist could alter Marsha's isolated upbringing or her catastrophic divorce. The challenge was to help her perceive in depth the fact that God and human experience were not to be judged by her unfortunate background. In a word, her belief system had to be dealt with. Male or female, young or old, isolation such as hers was impossible in the most important sense. The psalmist expressed the very sense she needed to capture: "Whither shall I flee from Thy presence?" (139:7). What people had failed to do for her, God was more than willing to do if she would open herself to God's care.

Because of her previous intellectual curiosity and wide readings, Marsha found guided meditations rewarding. They also prevented her from engaging in threatening social contacts before she was ready. She conceived of and then slowly moved to meet the God who is present in all experience and turns it to blessing. She experienced this God first in sunsets and forms of new life in springtime. These experiences were fail-safe, because they did not depend on the adequacy of performers other than the therapist. She responded well, both in her meditative disciplines and in the reduction of her symptoms. Her life brightened to the point where she was caught in several spontaneous and radiant smiles.

It was time, now, to branch out from her inward emphasis and her overdependence on the therapist. This required placement in a group, which was difficult because of her wide reading and free thinking. She did not fit into the typical church group that might have provided the dependable warmth that she needed. However, the therapist was aware of a religious group that claimed to have no prescribed doctrines. They were open to all faith styles, and yet were trying to establish a utopian type of warm community, not unlike a more traditional church. An older woman in the group started this phase of the healing process by inviting Marsha to a concert. The therapist recommended that she accept, which she did, with surprisingly pleasant results. As the new group reached out to her, Marsha found it more and more difficult to feel as alone as she was accustomed to feeling. It was a bit disturbing at first, but it was also enjoyable.

The focus of the meditations had been shifted from God in nature to God in people. This laid the foundations for the increase, little by little, of Marsha's contact with the group. When the contracted twenty sessions were completed, Marsha was not a social butterfly, but she was symptom-free most of the time. She was growing increasingly through her own direction and initiative.

Case 15

Terri, age twenty-six, was also beset by symptoms beyond the reach of her general practice physician, who referred her to the clinic. In addition to her shortness of breath, "pounding of the heart," and cold sweats, her presenting symptoms included a bizarre and constant fear of being attacked. She was not paranoid about people as such, but she was intensively defensive and on guard. She was easily startled and never ever really rested in her sleep. In a word, life for Terri could not be trusted, nor, by implication, could its Creator.

She had been nervous and easily frightened all her life. Her sense of impending danger had been evident even when she was an infant in the crib. This was probably the result of an extremely difficult birth. Her early panic syndrome was intensified by the fact that her mother, a strong, dominating person, appeared not to accept her. Since neither her father nor any surrogate parent ever seriously tried to make up the deficit in affection, it mounted daily. Every time her mother roared an order, it promoted panic. Thus when her mother discovered her curiously exploring sex difference with a small boy, the judgmental outburst left Terri with the deep impression that all physical interest and desire were "of the devil." At age seven, Terri was found innocently daydreaming, whereupon her mother solemnly ordered her never to let her mind relax, since "an idle mind is Satan's workshop."

When Terri was eight, her father gave up on the marriage, and her mother was glad, since he had been much "too interested in fleshly things." There was thus established in Terri's mind a firm dichotomy between flesh and spirit, with sexuality relegated to the side of evil flesh. The trouble was that she was both curious and attractive, and she found it impossible to follow her mother's rigid mandates. Beginning in her teens, Terri experimented with sex, always looking over her shoulder in fear. Each relationship would begin, as she put it, "nice," and then "wickedness" would set in, with her "enjoying bad things" to keep the relationship going. Her pangs of conscience were dulled only by alcohol or some other form of substance abuse. It was a marvel that this had not led to regular addiction rather than her strictly occasional indulgence.

Two husbands had reluctantly divorced her because they were not capable of meeting her strange pattern of needs. They found it impossible to cope with her involuntary and at times apologetic tenseness. Her startled and terrified response to almost any sound made life with her almost unbearable, even without her periodic explosions. It would have been easy enough to accept a third husband, since there were plenty of candidates. But she knew that her restlessness and fitful outbursts would have led to still another divorce. Also, her headaches and cold sweats were getting worse, not better.

Terri's regimen of treatment was coordinated with her referring physician, who gradually reduced her medications. She went through the disciplines of physical relaxation, without which other therapy would have made no impact. This posed problems for Terri, since her body was already the declared enemy. Likewise, the standard prayer disciplines met with subtle resistance, born of the fact that Terri's God was as mean and demanding as her mother. She had stayed away from "Him" as much as possible. Thus she required intense belief system therapy.

Terri needed first to gain an intellectual assent and then a deep intuitive affirmation that God is good and that all of creation, including the human body, is good. Terri's mother had based her gross miseducation on her own strange, warped ideas and her enjoyment of negative authority. This view was so deeply ingrained that Terri opened up only slowly to the positive teaching of the Bible. In addition to the usual word about the goodness of creation (Gen. 1:31), the therapist used God's command to Peter (Acts 10:15), which he paraphrased to read, "Don't you call anything I made unclean!" The intellectual agreement came fairly easily, but emotional habits and intuitive learnings of a lifetime are not so easy to break. This required many sessions of relaxed listening to the taped affirmations, in spoken and musical art forms or worship. It also required more than the usual counseling appointments before real progress was evident. Terri still had a long way to go when her months of treatment were finished.

For every such tragic case as those related above, there are likely hundreds that never receive any type of professional help. So many people assume that God is good and life is not. In deeper levels of consciousness, the two are inseparable. The celebration of life and the praise of God are two sides of the same coin, and both are indispensable to wholeness. God surely does not need human praise, but the praise blesses the praiser.

The leftover philosophies of the Greek Stoic reformation still reign, little checked, so far, by recent brilliant clinical insights. The more prevalent voice in too many minds is that of the Apostle Paul crying, "For I know that in me [that is in my flesh] dwelleth no good thing" (Rom. 7:18). All too faint is the voice of the psalmist singing, "I will praise Thee, for I am fearfully and wonderfully made" (139:14). Too few people take the doctrine of the Imago Dei seriously, leading to the certain need for a new emphasis on the goodness of God and creation. Such a wedding would match the newly enlightened holism of medicine and ministry. Few affirmations are more essential to spiritual wholeness and emotional health than the dual belief in the goodness of God and creation. It is no figment of an unorthodox therapist's mind; it is the very message of the Bible, ever since God looked at creation and declared that it was good. It has been tested and found to be sound on the continent of Africa and in all the rest of the earth.

7. The Grace of God

"For by grace are ye saved [and acceptable] through faith." (Eph. 2:8)

The sixth and climactic divine attribute and affirmation in the Soul system of belief is that God is gracious. The crowning and ultimate trait of the Eternal is understanding forgiveness or unconditional, unmerited acceptance. One's evil deeds must be healthily confronted and repented, to be sure, but no amount of sin renders one unacceptable, if one can believe the good news of the gospel. Persons do not earn acceptance with God; it is a *gift*. Furthermore, the love and acceptance offered by family or true friends must also be given freely to be called love. This mediates and is one way of making real the crowning characteristic of God.

The grace of God is the pinnacle point of theology and therapy, of Christian faith and of spiritual and emotional wholeness. The Bible record is rightfully referred to as "salvation [acceptability] history," and the entire New Testament records the reconciliation of humanity to God through the life and death of Jesus Christ. This inaugurated the era of grace, following the era of Old Testament law and justice. Therapeutically speaking, the parallel is the establishment, in human understanding, of God's unconditional acceptance. Based on God's appraisal, it is possible to engage in healthy human self-esteem. For the hereafter and the here, the grace of God offers unqualified love: freedom from divine condemnation and from neurotic dependence on the approval or acceptance of others.

The question immediately arises: how on earth did such good news become so prevalent in a slave society, especially since slavery was precisely designed to promulgate the opposite? Where would a bondservant look for unconditional love in a system controlled by whips and pistols? Overseers were carefully taught never to appear pleased, even with the best of work, or of workers as persons. The answer lies once again in an ingenious and providential synthesis of African religious and cultural roots with an amazingly accurate grasp of Scripture.

The grace of God flourished in the slave quarter, in part, because it had obviously parallel roots in Africa. It was not the singular or central idea of traditional African belief, but it was definitely manifest in the praise names for High God. Many people hold a popular African stereotype of superstitious efforts to please gods believed to be far more demanding and cruel than gracious. This constitutes, at best, a gross misreading of their positive world view and life-celebrating culture. The Yoruba called High God "A Alanu," the Merciful God, and "Olore," the Benefactor, the Well-Doer. The Ashanti had a name for God literally meaning, "He who causes rain to fall on all copiously," and the symbolism of this name "Totrobonsu" concerned the generosity and magnanimity of God. It resembled the rain figure used in Matthew declaring that God graciously causes the rain to fall on the just and the unjust (5:45). Clearly the graciousness of God was no startling revelation to the African mind.

African proverbs also testified to God's grace. The Yoruba said, "If God should compute our sins, we should all perish." The entire corpus of African expressions about Providence are also closely akin to grace.

It is therefore not strange that early American Soul songs, or spirituals, should have included an assortment of affirmations of God's graciousness, each in a different concrete situation. When slavery looked hopeless, Blacks still sang, "Didn't my Lord deliver Daniel, and why not every man?" Implying also God's Omnipotence and justice they sang, "O, Mary, don't you weep, don't you mourn. . . . Pharaoh's army got drownded." Speaking directly of the spirit of grace, they sang, "There is a balm in Gilead, to make the wounded whole; There is a balm in

Gilead, to heal the sin-sick soul." In this same vein of graciousness, but without the Western emphasis on the "sin-sickness,"
Blacks sang, "Swing low, sweet chariot, comin' for to carry me
home," and "'Tis the ole ship of Zion. . . . It has landed many
a thousand. . . . The fare is cheap an' all can ride; the rich an'
poor are there; no second class aboard this train, no difference
in the fare." The gracious deliverance from the oppressions and
sufferings of this earth was symbolized in each song, a grace
that is not based on any consideration of merit.

The most forthright expression of the Soul system's belief in
grace was to be found, however, in the choice of hymns appropriated. There is no doubt that the favorite by far was and is
"Amazing Grace." Its stanzas also include:

'Twas grace that taught my heart to fear,
    And grace my fears relieved;
How precious did that grace appear,
    The hour I first believed.
Through many dangers, toils and snares,
    I have already come;
'Tis grace that brought me safe thus far,
    And grace will lead me home.

(John Newton)

Another very popular hymn by Robert Robinson, "Come, Thou
Fount of Every Blessing," contains the declaration, "O to grace
how great a debtor, daily I'm constrained to be. . . ." Aside
from these favorites, almost any popular hymn is likely to contain a reference if not a whole stanza about grace. For instance,
one stanza of "My Faith Looks Up to Thee" begins: "May thy
rich grace impart strength to my fainting heart" (Ray Palmer).
The idea of grace is inescapable in the second most popular
hymn in the Black church: Joseph Scriven's "What a friend we
have in Jesus, all our sins and griefs to bear." Clearly, Black
hymnody speaks often of God's grace.

The modern tradition of gospel songs in Soul worship similarly focuses often on the grace of God. Indeed, the concept

takes on a kind of personhood, with lines such as Roberta Martin's, "Grace woke me up this morning . . . started me on my way." Grace and Providence are blended in the lines from Clarence Cobb, "Soul looked back and wondered how I got over." The goodness and grace of God are implicit in many songs already discussed under other doctrines. When one sings, "He'll understand, and say, 'Well done,' " (Lucie Campbell) the implications are not limited to omniscience. God's grace is implied also in these lines from Isaiah Jones, quoted on the goodness of God: "I don't deserve all of this good; so many things are not as they should be, but God is so good to me." Gospel songs abundantly speak of undeserved blessings, or God's grace.

The pervasiveness of grace in the hymns and gospel songs is not accidental; it is easily apparent in the Bible record on which they are all based. For instance, Joseph sums up his story saying, "God meant it for good" (Gen. 50:19–20). While the usual reading of this passage rightly emphasizes Providence, it is also clear that Joseph was able to forgive his brothers through grace. The theme surfaces in Deuteronomy with a combination of poetic ingenuity and African animal symbolism. Israel's chronic failure to follow God's will is likened to eagles learning to fly, with the mother eagle poised to rescue them in case they falter (Deut. 32:11). The mother eagle symbolizes the merciful Jehovah of the Old Testament.

The Psalms are rich in references to God's mercy. One Hebrew word for mercy appears in them sixty-seven times, such as in this favorite passage: "The Lord is merciful and gracious, slow to anger, and plenteous in mercy" (103:8). Still another Hebrew word for mercy appears twelve times, as in the classic plea, "Have mercy upon me, O God, according to Thy lovingkindness; according unto the multitude of Thy tender mercies blot out my transgressions" (51:1). Psalms 106 and 107 begin with a formula that includes the same word, illustrating a major theme of the whole Hebrew hymnbook: "O give thanks unto the Lord; for he is good: for his mercy endureth forever."

The prophets abound in illustrations of God's mercy. The

Servant Songs of Isaiah show God's intent to restore the erring tribes of Jacob and to use them to bring light to the Gentiles (49:6). In Ezekiel, God promises to put in people a new spirit (36:26), and the book of Hosea tells a story of unmerited acceptance. The book of Jonah provides prophetic satire: a gracious God saves Nineveh despite the preacher's reluctance and fierce unforgiveness. Throughout the entire Old Testament, God tries to reach humanity with mercy or grace more than judgment.

In the New Testament, the incarnation reveals God's ultimate effort to accomplish reconciliation. The parable of the cruel vinedressers (Matt. 21:33–41; Mark 12:1–9; Luke 20:9–16) suggests this event as the last in a series of attempts to reconcile erring humanity. The Apostle Paul aptly captioned it in 2 Corinthians: "God was in Christ, reconciling the world unto himself, not imputing their trespasses unto them: and hath committed unto us the word of reconciliation" (5:19).

The parables speak most graphically of God's grace without ever using the word. The gracious "householder" (vineyard-keeper) pays the latecomers for a full day's work (Matt. 20:1–16). The friend at midnight (Luke 11:5–13) and the importunate widow (Luke 18:1–8) are seeking unmerited mercy and receiving it. The trilogy of the lost sheep, the lost coin, and the lost son portrays a gracious, seeking God (Luke 15). The most effective and important statement of the whole New Testament may very well be the attitude of the forgiving father, which is the primary meaning of the parable of the lost son.

Grace is contrasted with the law throughout the voluminous correspondence of the Apostle Paul. A typical example is found in his theological summary written to the Romans: "For all have sinned, and come short of the glory of God; being justified freely by his grace through the redemption that is in Christ Jesus" (3:23–24). The theme of grace dominates in the Bible.

The major challenge in life is to move the grace of God from the role of attractive abstraction to relevant reality, perceived and felt in the depths of human consciousness. The tragic fact is that, wittingly or unwittingly, religious institutions have historically compromised grace. The Protestant Reformation was launched in an effort to stop the selling of "indulgences," a system of prepaid forgiveness dispensed by the church. Martin Luther's powerful proclamation, "For by Grace are ye saved through faith" (Eph. 2:8), was designed to rescue forgiveness from fundraising. He was trying to restore the original good news of free grace, or God's unconditional acceptance.

Nevertheless, this is not to be confused with what twentieth-century theologian Dietrich Bonhoeffer called "cheap grace." As Paul put it, "Shall we continue in sin, that grace may abound? God forbid!" (Rom. 6:1–2) Rather, while the emphasis here may seem one-sided, it is compensatory and temporary in order to be therapeutic. It is designed to shatter the grip of the demon of conditional acceptance. Once one accepts in depth the good news that the grace of God is not in fact too good to be true, then the ethical elaborations of being accepted or saved may be addressed. Before that, one is immobilized and alienated, unable to love the God who has already loved us (1 John 4:19). Granted grace, one can move on to growth in maturity and responsibility.

The matured human spirit, in its integrity, resists cheap grace. Practitioners who seek to heal guilt by dissolving the moral code find even immature people resisting this technique. People sense intuitively the dangers of a world without ethical guidelines. In 1961, a therapist named O. Hobart Mowrer spelled out the dangers of dismantling the social contract in order to relieve guilt in his book *The Crisis in Psychiatry and Religion*. He insisted that the confessions required in 1 John 1:8–9 were clinically justified in the experience of many, including members of Alcoholics Anonymous: "If we say that we have no sin, we deceive ourselves, and the truth is not in us. If we confess our sins, he is faithful and just to forgive us our sins, and to cleanse us from all unrighteousness." Once this gracious forgiveness is received, Mowrer further stated, the person must make "every effort within his power to undo the evil for which he was previously responsible" (108). Grace, then, is not cheap, and effort at restitution is a signal of growth in both healthy self-esteem and mature responsibility.

Jesus' parable of the unmerciful servant powerfully underscores the effect of a negative response to the offer of grace (Matt. 18:21–35). In this story, the king's forgiveness of debt is revoked because of the servant's failure to be likewise forgiving of one who had owed him a much smaller debt. Indeed, in graciousness is the only reliable evidence of grace received, whether theologically (cf. the Epistle of James) or therapeutically. One's level of faith is always reflected in gracious works and warm relationships.

This index of faith uncovers great gaps between the ability to sing about grace and an intuitive sense of acceptance in the clinical cases to which we now turn. This is more than mere misunderstanding of the rhetoric in the songs. People hope for grace, but it is too good to be true at their deep levels of consciousness, formed by the presence or absence of grace in experience, or true community. Yet the songs and sayings of the faith and culture represent resources that provide help by simply being there and presenting a vision. The task of the helpers in church and clinic is to make more real and healing the faith so richly affirmed in the very culture that also often denies grace in practice.

The four following cases show less than desirable progress into outgoing, gracious relations with others, simply because people lacking a sense of God's grace seldom get that far in therapy. The treatment merely opens the way for true discipleship by unlocking the prisons of guilt through the mediation of understanding grace. After being warmed and empowered by God's gracious love, the healing process can continue on to joyous discipleship, mature responsibility, and satisfying self-fulfillment in service. However, making real the latent possibilities in the cultural assurances of the grace of God is a fruitful first step.

Case 16

Charles, age nineteen, a hefty man, was dangerously tense
and under stress as he engaged in endless efforts to earn acceptance. This ambitious young athlete was willing to do anything
to succeed and please others, so his coach met no resistance
when he suggested that Charles seek the advice of a sports
therapist. On his first appointment, Charles frankly reported
his constant feeling of stress that appeared to have no reason.
He was also chronically fatigued, despite his large muscles and
powerful appearance. He was plagued by the feeling that he
simply wasn't "good enough" in either sports or morals. In
fact, any time he caught himself having fun, he felt guilty, no
matter how innocent the activity. He would have liked to see
himself a winner, but he always seemed to be a loser, at home,
school, and work. He was diagnosed as having depressive
neurosis.

In the case history, Charles recalled that already at age four,
he could not please his father. His mother had to protect him
from his father's bad fits of temper. By the time he was seven,
he had decided he needed to be as tough as his father, an ambi-
tion he found impossible, since he tended to cry "too easily."
By the time he was ten he was infected with chauvinism: "I
tried to get rid of the girlish things in me." At fifteen Charles
had been angry at both the world and himself, profoundly
afraid, and convinced that nobody loved him.

His repressed anger at the cruel world was dangerous even
in his own sight. He wanted to kill anyone who hurt him. He
thought better of it, of course, because, "With my luck I feared
I'd end up dead myself instead." His living epitaph at age nineteen was, "If I were ever really to let go and be myself, I'd die."
In effect he was already dead.

Charles's treatment started with disciplines of physical relaxation, which served as a bridge to feelings of emotional calm.
During these states he was led to identify the messages of
inadequacy that had plagued him from early childhood. In

truth, it appeared that his father's disappointed sports ambitions had not been a major factor, and Charles's demands had been mostly self-inflicted. Emotional habits this old were not easily erased, but at least Charles had the advantage of not having to remove anyone else from his subconsciousness.

The theme of the affirmations commended to him was taken from Charlotte Elliott's old hymn, "Just as I am, without one plea. . . . And that thou bidst me come to thee. . . ." He was also reassured with Paul's declaration that *all* people are saved and accepted by grace; people are not approved on their own achievements (Eph. 2:8–9). Charles began slowly to sense that *perhaps* he was "good enough," after all. He began to hold up his head and relax; the two went together. At the same time, Charles was guided to engage in noncompetitive physical fitness, as opposed to team sports focused on winning. In this outlet free of demand, his performance improved markedly. The relaxed action was satisfying in a way he had never experienced while using exercise for recognition. Obviously he was not an outstanding athlete, but this was beginning to be all right. The therapist helped him avoid trying too hard, either in exercise or in efforts to believe in the grace of God.

With the self-made pressures released, Charles found he had more energy and stopped feeling the unexplainable fatigue. His work and studies all showed improvement. His faithful participation in thirty-two sessions had paid off, and he had mastered disciplines that would facilitate growth for years to come. The grace of God and the acceptance of therapist and coach were linked realities which soothed and healed him. He was even willing now to take their advice that life was supposed to be abundant, and he let himself begin enjoying it.

Case 17

Jannette's desperate need for gracious acceptance began at her birth twenty-four years earlier, but she was not aware of this when she came to the therapist. Her visit had been prompted by her community college counselor, when it had been discovered that she was flunking despite good intelligence scores. Her symptoms included a loss of appetite, unhealthy loss of weight, problems with trying to sleep, and a massive depression. She had no energy, and she found it impossible to make up her mind about almost everything. "It's a wonder I made it to this office," she said. Her catalog of horrors included the inability to enjoy anything at all, even her formerly favorite activities. Instead of feeling rested in the morning, she found it her worst time of the day. At bottom she wished she were dead.

Jannette's background left no doubt as to how she had landed in such hard emotional straits. An unwanted baby, she had been nearly strangled in delivery by her own umbilical cord. Her mother's maternal instincts had not overcome her prenatal attitude, and she had hated the baby so much she found it impossible to breast-feed her. Jan recalled being told from an early age that her mother's life would have been much happier without her, and that, in fact, she may have been a kind of curse to punish her mother for her sins.

Thus stigmatized, the child had been isolated in her own family. As a twelve-year-old, she was sexually abused by her stepfather, whose threats protected his assaults until she was sixteen. Then her mother's discovery only landed Jan in a Catholic boarding school "to have her sinful nature taken away." The stepfather was hardly reprimanded. Less than two years later, she was expelled for bad grades and put on her own, utterly traumatized by the absurdity of the treatment given her. Within six months she had had two abortions and was tempted to agree with her family's evil opinion of her character. Pregnant again the next year, she tried to follow the church's guidance by giving birth and putting the child up for adoption. Nevertheless, she contracted genital herpes in what she saw as punishment for her former sins. She now believed herself to be a dangerous source of infection, a person whose accidental touch could cause such calamities as blindness. She was close to committing suicide, but instead she vowed to change her life.

Jan's survival instinct paid off. In a little over a year, she had completed high school equivalency and started the long, slow trek through college on a part-time basis. She was doing fairly well, earning her way and making good grades, when she was overtaken by complete physical and emotional exhaustion. At twenty-four she was overloaded and overcome by hopelessness and depression. All this might have destroyed her at twenty, but now she simply delivered herself to the clinic.

Her impressive determination helped her make the best of therapy, and her arduous cooperation yielded limited results where failure would have been certain otherwise. The relaxation disciplines were very difficult for Jan. The instinct for struggle developed at birth resulted in a tense readiness not easily surrendered after twenty-four years. She had to be slowly convinced at deep levels that God was not poised to pounce on her every mistake, so it was safe to relax. There was also a need to undermine, bit by bit, her view of herself as sinful and deserving of such surveillance. God was shown to her to be "slow to anger and plenteous in mercy" (Ps. 103:8).

Jan was taught and then deeply impressed with the fact that there was a difference between being and doing, what one is as opposed to what one does. Her *being* had always been in God's image (Gen. 1:26), and her *doing* was capable of being changed. This was especially true now that she was free from the family's abuses and could understand their part in her mistakes. She could be thankful for her will to struggle, which was a miracle under the circumstances.

Jannette's need for forgiveness was slow to be satisfied. Given the atrocities she had suffered, the therapist believed she needed not so much forgiveness as a raised self-esteem. He nevertheless honored her hunger for what in the traditional liturgy is referred to as "assurance of pardon." The repertoire of affirmative prescriptions included the passage in 1 John 1 that promises God is "faithful and just to forgive" those who confess (8–9). This was backed up musically with the third stanza of Thomas O. Chisholm's "Great Is Thy Faithfulness," which promises, "Pardon for sin and a peace that endureth. . . . Strength for today and bright hope for tomorrow. . . ." She was particularly fond of a choral anthem singing J. B. Roberts's setting of Isaiah's words:

Seek ye the Lord while he may be found,
    Call ye upon him while he is near;
    Let the wicked forsake his way,
And the unrighteous man his thoughts;
    And let him return unto the Lord . . .
    And he will have mercy upon him:
And to Our God, for he will abundantly pardon. . . . (55:6–7)

She played that cassette repeatedly at home, singing along with the choir and feeling her spirit soar. As her sense of pardon ran deeper, she was more and more impressed with her inner capacity to extend the divine pardon to others. The new church she attended helped greatly, and the pastor impressed on her the fact that the God she had feared desired for her "life, and that more abundantly" (John 10:10). Jan's schoolwork improved markedly, and her sense of physical well-being increased with participation in required physical education. At the end of therapy she even ran for class office. She did not win, but she was surprised at how many voted for her. They, like God, had accepted her by grace.

Three months of work had paid off, and she promised to send the therapist notes from time to time regarding her progress. The church and pastor and school counselor would all continue to help, and she would be their helper as well. Most of all, she could feel even better about herself because she was pardoned and accepted by the grace of God.

Case 18

Connie also viewed God as mean, and, typically, her life was haunted by a sense of gross inadequacy and imperfection. She was an intermittent alcoholic and abuser of medications. Although forty-two years old, she exhibited persistent childishness—stark terror at the thought that her mother might not love her, a fear that she could not possibly "make it" on her own, and a set of impossibly perfectionist demands guaranteeing her failure. She felt like she was under scrutiny or "on TV" all the time, and she kept an absolutely spotless house and clothing. Yet she hated the fact that she felt so watched.

As she unfolded her case history, she was plagued by the idea that her sins were utterly unique and beyond forgiveness. She felt she had invented them. So she was rather disappointed when the therapist carefully avoided showing any judgmental reactions. Heightened response would have fed her subtle need to stir up anger or reproof. Since this was the best form of care she had ever received, she was slow to understand that the therapist cared in a more complete and helpful way.

The oldest of seven children, Connie had been expected to be the perfect model for the others. She had ducked the responsibility by subterfuge, using childish ways and good looks in order to avoid her parents' purposes. It had worked too well, so that they had discouraged even the few times she had tried to be independent. Trapped in her own disguise, she had spent the rest of her life keeping it in working order. She felt no genuine respect from anybody, but she was haunted by the need to be perfect enough to deserve it anyway.

Other factors further undermined her self-esteem. When Connie was thirteen, her mother had found her masturbating, advised her that it was dirty, and ordered her never to do it again. Shortly thereafter, she had been deeply impressed by a sermon in which the human body was characterized as the "temple of God," The preacher had condemned "dirty" things: "We must keep God's house clean, or else!" Connie therefore perceived God as just as demanding as her mother. This did not deter her from a single, fearful experiment with sex two years later, which may have enhanced her fascination with the subject but destroyed all enjoyment. She had never experimented again, but she also never forgave herself. These two incidents hung like a cloud over her spirit. Her fits of awesome unworthiness had only increased in the following twenty-one years. When they were unbearable, she resorted to medications or alcohol, resulting in the dangers that drove her to the clinic.

The therapist immediately contacted her physician, and they arranged a gradual withdrawal of the drugs she was taking. Then began the main task of helping her to escape the control of other people and substances. To take responsibility for herself she needed a radically different belief system, free of a God whose meanness duplicated her parents' demanding and conditional acceptance. The other side of this coin was her own self-made perfectionist demands. She was doomed by her own requirements. She needed to meet and build trust in the God of grace, the heavenly parent who only requires that we keep trying and trusting.

Soon after the preliminary exams and exercises, the therapist asked Connie to enter into acting out a play. He was to be a little child who was learning to walk, and she was to be the parent. Her role was to spank him every time he fell down and every time he refused to leave hold of the chair and try. Connie found this all quite impossible to do and indeed ridiculous. Then suddenly she understood the significance of the exercise. It was just as ridiculous to believe that the God the Bible talks about was angry with her, when she had tried so hard and failed.

The Bible yielded many correctives for her beliefs. The therapist told her stories like the parable of the forgiving father (Luke 15:11–24) and had her listen repeatedly to these tapes. She memorized 1 John 1:8–9: "He is faithful and just to forgive us our sins, and to cleanse us from all unrighteousness." Then she listened to hymns such as "Amazing Grace," which reinforced her new vision of a gracious God.

Connie received much comfort from the Apostle Paul's discussion of his "thorn in the flesh" (2 Cor. 12:7–9). She was amazed that a famous saint like Paul had to depend on grace also. It was a bit easier now to accept her weakness, even if she could not honestly say that she gloried in it as did Paul. She learned, with Paul, that to face weakness and trust a gracious God at the same time is strength.

Connie began to accept the care shown by her therapist, and in doing so, she tasted the profound acceptance that God also was extending to her. She began to understand that her mother's manipulative kind of love had never been real love in the first place. The housework that was a key to her mother's approval now easily explained her present compulsion for spot-lessness. Understanding this she began to break the habit of trying to please everyone. The God of grace had accepted her already, by faith.

Connie had to stop her treatment after twenty sessions, but she was already capable of relaxing and free of dependence on medications and alcohol. She had come so far that she was willing to risk being responsible for herself as an adult. She was well on her way to knowing that God's grace was adequate to help her cope.

The most widespread weakness in the ministry of Christian churches today may well be the failure adequately to teach and mediate the grace of God. It may also be that this is a major contributing factor to the high percentage of need shown by persons seeking clinical help. Although the cases here clearly show the potential value of churches as healing networks of support, the record to date has not convinced most clinicians of the value of a partnership with the churches.

The verbal basis for belief in the grace of God is still very much alive in the culture of Protestant America. The problem is to translate the rhetoric of hymns into deep assurance at the intuitive level. Two types of people feel the greatest need: (1) those who have migrated away from a soulful culture base, or faith, and (2) members of churches which for theological or strategic (manipulative) reasons tend to keep people feeling guilty. The burden of this chapter and indeed of this entire book is to challenge both leaders and laity to become the mediators of grace which only the household of faith can be to the fullest possibilities of healing. No person or church committed to ministry in the name of Christ, the literal embodiment of God's grace, can dare do less.

8. The Equality of Persons

"There is neither Jew nor Greek, there is neither bond nor free, there is neither male nor female; for ye are all one in Christ Jesus." (Gal. 3:28)

Alongside the affirmations of Soul theology dealing with attributes of God are also some key beliefs dealing more directly with humanity. The first of four such affirmations with great power is the intrinsic equality of all persons. The way the doctrine is stated may vary from "egalitarianism," a term used in academia, to "no big I's and little you's," as heard on the streets of the Soul community. Its best-known form, taken from neither place, is in the Preamble to the United States Constitution: "We hold these truths to be self-evident, that all men are created equal, and that they are endowed by their Creator with certain inalienable rights. . . ." This is the very foundation of American democracy; all political structures and activity are based on the ideal of "one person, one vote." Yet few have stopped to think how important this same concept is theologically, or how, like all true theology, it also undergirds the psychic and spiritual wholeness of persons.

Equality is not merely political rhetoric; it involves God's justice expressed impartially. Either God regards all persons as intrinsically equal, or this Deity is the unjust author of inequity, the very Creator of the oppressions suffered by persons and groups at the bottom of the social and economic system. As easy as it may be to practice inequality, the American dream will not permit it to be approved by the Creator. Only in inferior belief systems such as Nazism or Fascism can the Deity condone arbitrary distinctions. The founders of this nation attributed their egalitarian dogma to the very mind of God, and so Americans have believed ever since.

This equality is not to be mistaken for uniformity, however. Americans come in differing sizes and shapes. They have various levels of giftedness, in a further diversified spectrum of specialties. They represent a fantastic variety of colors and cultures, from every corner of the earth, to say nothing of a profusion of personality patterns. Still, before the law, they are equal in standing. Few affirmations have more sweeping consequences, psychologically and spiritually as well as legally, and few are so inadequately articulated, especially in America's circles of power. The pluralism of the dream is far better understood today than ever, but the drift toward the tyranny of single-group supremacy and enforced uniformity is always present.

Despite these failures of idealism, the Soul culture offers impressive examples of a profound belief in the dream of equality. With equality still so widely denied after over three and a half centuries in this country, one wonders how it was ever grasped in the first place and held so tenaciously. The answer becomes clear, however, if one looks in the right places: (1) Equality was and is deeply imbedded in African culture and society, widespread and supposedly scholarly stereotypes to the contrary notwithstanding. (2) The Bible espouses equality quite forcefully in places, in addition to numerous passages where it is implied. (3) The very ability to survive in wholeness under massive cruelty in a closed society requires that one believe that his or her plight is contrary to the very will of God. Examples of the first two follow.

Like much of the belief system held by expatriate Africans, equality arrived on these shores in the hearts and minds of Black slaves. African cultural declarations of equality ranged from the lofty rhetoric of proverbial wisdom to a system of ritual insult. The equality of persons was often symbolized in the uniform inescapability of death. One proverb states that medical doctors and fetish priests alike will all die, and that their consultants will not be left behind either. Another figure suggests that inequality is unnecessary, because "the sky is big enough for any number of birds." Another appeals to the common source of the gift of life, saying, "All men are the children of the Supreme Being; no one is a child of the earth." This equality is flawed, of course, by the lower status accorded women, as in the first versions of the American dream, but the basic notion is unmistakable.

African culture also provided a clever equalizer that anthropologists call "ritual insult." If one had a grievance against a neighbor, a third party was enlisted to receive an unmerciful scolding related to that offense. This took place in the carefully arranged presence of the offender who, as eavesdropper, dared not interfere. The offender was not spoken to, yet he or she dared not leave and miss the message. This guarantee of a forum for redress applied, in many tribes, even when the offender was the king or chief. Once a year one could scold the king with complete immunity. The tradition of some tribes even prescribed suicide for tyrants, to avoid leaders who loved too much power. The alternative was an uninvestigated homicide, since traditional culture treasured freedom and knew that living ekings always had trouble giving up their special privileges. Thus African culture, at its best, left none voiceless or arbitrarily unequal, and it systematically avoided dictators.

In American Black culture of church and street the ritual insult survives in a practice called *signifying*. With or without an uninvolved third party as dummy hearer, frank complaints can be voiced in a privileged setting. "Some people say" or "I heard" may introduce the issue, while the offender who objects or defends may be told, "Ain't nobody talking to [or about] you," or a stinging, "If the shoe fits, wear it." Assignment to a lowly status has not succeeded in convincing Blacks to dismantle their ancient and egalitarian system of redress by verbal indirection.

This example of the Soul commitment to personal parity is part of a much larger whole. It is manifest in spirituals and churches, but also in street culture, where it receives an equal if not greater cultural commitment. Personal parity is seen in this example of a West Coast construction laborer's relationship to his mostly unemployed associates on the block. He treasured his identity as just one of the bunch, but he was much more resourceful than they. A few years earlier, he had bought a cheap hillside lot which had increased in value beyond his fondest dreams. Instead of selling it, he had scrounged enough scrap and surplus materials from job sites to help him complete a near-mansion in the heights, using the traded weekend labor of craftsmen from his jobs. Everybody on the block knew of his success, but he dared not mention it to them lest he seem up-pity. When rare mention of it was made by others, equality demanded that he remain most humble. Further, all the time spent with his friends had to be on their block and nobody felt hurt that he had the good sense not to invite them up to his house. Yet all had sneaked up the hill to satisfy their curiosity. The block remained the one haven where self-respect and equality were not at risk; it was the successor to the early African village whose equality lingered in a nostalgic collective consciousness. On that block and hundreds like it nobody was an outcast, regardless of deformity, insanity, criminal record, or addiction, so long as she or he gave equal respect to others.

The spirituals that evolved during the years of slavery reflect similar certainty of the equality of persons. They often expressed it in the context of heaven, but this was not escapism. It was safe discourse in the midst of White censors and a clear declaration of the ultimate state of things as they are in heaven and should be on earth. Thus the famous spiritual about having shoes in heaven emphasizes equality: "All God's children got shoes." One could paraphrase the rest to say, "When I get to heaven, I plan to exercise my equality and express myself all over heaven, without restriction."

Not a single widely known spiritual so much as hints at less than ultimate equality. Even the famous "Live Humble"* was not an expression of belief in inferiority. Rather, it was a hidden warning to look humble before masters, because bloody

---

*"Live-a humble, humble, humble, Lord; Humble yo'self, de bell done rung."

repression had been instituted after the Nat Turner Rebellion. The "bell done rung" signalled sensitivity to slave resistance. Another spiritual proclaimed equality in the dining room: "I'm gonna *sit* at the welcome table one of these days." A spiritual prayed, "Lord I want to be more loving," referring to White masters also, but it never implied acceptance of their sinful system.

Two other very famous spirituals express the slave insistence on equality in powerful, direct terms. One was widely sung during the 1960s in the great civil rights campaigns: "And before I'd be a slave [in my heart] I'd be buried in my grave, and go home to my Lord and be free." The other, already quoted in a previous chapter, is the well-known spiritual about the Gospel Train:

The fare is cheap, and all can ride, the rich and poor are there.
No second class aboard this train, no difference in the fare.
Oh, get on board, little children, get on board, little children,
Get on board, little children, there's room for many a'more.

The African Americans survived in part because of a profound and unshakable confidence that God did not will them to be enshackled or considered unequal.

Although slaves were hardly allowed to read the Bible, they knew that the Bible, like their root culture, was loaded with support for the equality of persons. Their underground network of literates spread the word that God shows no respect for race or class (Acts 10:34–35). This quotation of Peter was based in turn on so early a passage as Deuteronomy 10:17. In the Old Testament, the entire book of Jonah stands as a prophetic statement against the Jewish prejudice toward non-Jews. The satire there portrays the preacher as hating the Ninevites so much that he is angry at the thought of their being saved, even by his own preaching. Isaiah described an ideal world in which the eyes of the blind are opened, the ears of the deaf unstopped, and the lame man leaps as a hart (35:1–10). The ring of equal blessing in the rule of God is impossible to miss.

The greatest Old Testament evidence for equality, however,

was its most important story, the Exodus. In the world of Soul theology, Moses is not so much a lawgiver as an emancipator. Because God used Moses to lead the children of Israel out of slavery, Moses was more important than Jesus in the minds of many slaves prior to the careful communication of the whole gospel. The spiritual "Go Down, Moses" telling Pharaoh to "let my people go" was the single most direct attack on inequality to be found in the whole corpus of spirituals.

The New Testament shows Jesus taking firm stands for equality and against racial and religious supremacism. The Jewish vocation as chosen people had by Jesus' time deteriorated to mere privileged status, and Jesus often moved against it. In John 4 he casually violated the bigoted shunning of Samaritans by journeying through their territory. He committed additional violations by boldly conversing with a woman, and a morally questionable one at that. He further recognized this outcast race in the parable of the good Samaritan who helped the wounded traveler when respectable Jews would not. In Matthew Jesus paid a rare compliment to the faith of a Canaanite woman (15:28), and Luke records Jesus as taking a still greater risk when he said of a hated Roman master sergeant, "I have not found so great faith, no not in all Israel" (7:9). Jesus in his ministry clearly assigned intrinsic equality to all persons.

Peter's classic statement in Acts 10:34 that God is "no respecter of persons" has many New Testament counterparts. In 1 Corinthians 12 the figure of the human body is used to show that every single part is equally essential. The least respected or "uncomely" parts are frankly and specifically included. Paul further promotes equality in the well-known passages about ethnic groups. In Romans he declared his indebtedness to barbarians (nonspeakers of Greek) and people considered unwise (1:14). In Galatians the message comes out loud and clear:

For as many of you as have been baptized in Christ have put on Christ. There is neither Jew nor Greek, there is neither bond nor free, there is neither male nor female; for ye are all one in Christ (3:27–28).

Paul's letter to the Colossians includes the same credo, placing Jews after the Greeks and adding, "circumcision and uncircumcision" (3:11). These statements are clearly visions of the equality intended by God.

Even Paul's controversial word in Ephesians instructing slaves to obey their masters is actually only a means of gaining the readers' attention so he can deliver the punch line, which is that there is only one master, and that is God (6:5–9). The same can be said of the controversial statements on women and children. Once the writer was sure of being heard, he introduced fresh insight.

Finally, the Epistle of James speaks even more pointedly to the evils of inequality. It condemns the preferential treatment apparently accorded the wealthy in the seating in the house of God. It cites the law of love against degrading the poor and reverencing those with the best clothing. James says this is committing sin (2:1–9).

Seriously embracing arbitrary distinctions is also a form of mental and spiritual illness. When one sees oneself as either more or less than others, one is less than whole. A false sense of superiority may be more dangerous to society, as people idolize self, race, class, caste, or gender in the place of God. When males accept equality, they are relieved of the need to be all-competent and without vulnerability. They can release tears and seek their goals through healthy effort rather than deadly overloads. The gap between male and female life expectancies can be narrowed and the percentage of widows reduced. However, few idolaters of self ever have the wisdom to seek assistance of either a pastor or a therapist.

On the other hand, clinics are crowded with persons deficient in self-esteem. Theirs is the illness of inadequate belief in either God as impartial or self as inherently equal. Therapists are often called on to declare the good news of equality, but many fail to utilize the powerful doctrinal and biblical authority available for this healing enterprise.

The appearance of humility can mask deep heresy as well as

insidious disease. Clinicians often must challenge patients with questions like, "What makes *your* sin so special and unforgivable?" Or again, "Who gave you a patent on *that* passion?" People who believe that only their own sins are unforgivable have fallen into the doctrinal error of limiting God's grace in their own case but in no other. Perhaps the one unforgivable sin is defining oneself in a category beyond the reach of God.

Whatever one's station in life, psychic and spiritual wholeness require that one find a place where it is possible to be at ease and equal—a place to be accepted as somebody. Soul folk find such a place in their churches and communities. This need, of course, never appears in isolation or apart from other aspects of deficient core beliefs. The first case below highlights both the varied mixture of need and the critical role of equality in wholeness. The other cases focus more specifically on equality and inferiority.

Case 19

At age thirty-four Benny developed a desperate need for assurance of his equality with persons. He, of course, could not identify this need. He went to his counselor in stark terror about his temper. His most recent tantrum had so alarmed his housemates that some of them had had nightmares about his all-too-obvious potential for violence. He could have murdered someone in such a disturbed state, or he might have been killed in perfectly good conscience and valid self-defense. The most effective and immediate means of getting him and others out of danger was to relieve his painful and pervasive suspicion that others looked down on him as unequal.

The one person Benny trusted at all was his counselor, who was something of a surrogate parent. His case history started with the fact that he had been unmanageably aggressive since an early age. His constantly defensive and combative mood likely went all the way back to a traumatic birth. His parents had suspected that strangulation and oxygen deprivation had caused brain damage of some sort, but it had never been verified.

Benny had left home early, right after his father's death, and his career had included a number of trades, together with substance abuse, crime, and some brushes with the law. During his seventeen years on the street he had lived in many cities, and his wide range of experience included a car accident from which he was not supposed to have survived. One day it had finally dawned on him that he must be alive for some purpose, and he looked for a way to begin helping people. Since this would surely require college training, he enrolled at age thirty-three.

Benny's treatment required self-understanding first, and then willingness to cooperate in his own reconditioning. It would not be easy. He was caught in a difficult transition from an almost underworld street culture to campus life and the middle-class lifestyle he had scorned for years. At least some of his seemingly pathological aggression had been essential to surviving in his original setting. He needed time to make the deep and difficult switch. His cultural metamorphosis would take place in addition to diagnosis and therapy for profound personality disorders.

Benny's treatment moved quickly from the usual relaxation disciplines to cassettes for disciplining consciousness. When he became disenchanted with these, he was given some gospel songs sung by Black church choirs. These were much more to his liking, and few clients have been more diligent or delighted. The gospel songs kept him mindful of the Providence and grace of God, while he scrambled to survive on a very low budget, often without minimal pocket change.

Benny needed to develop as quickly as possible a strong inner assurance of divinely ordained and unconditional equality to lower his sensitivity to both real and imagined insults. He too easily suspected that people were ridiculing his uncouth background or his less-than-average height. Whether he dangerously vented his rage or heroically held it in, his anger threatened to make him sick and even self-destructive. He also risked triggering a return to substance abuse, the common solace for pain in his previous world. The strength of belief here was more than usually crucial.

Benny needed to see divinely ordained equality at work in the real world. He had to see that there were others who had left his kind of life and developed trades or professional skills which they were able to use later in very satisfying service. Benny learned that God had restored people who were at least as ill as he had been. The counselor found a church with a comfortable minority of former legal offenders, and Benny was warmly welcomed in. Being assigned tasks and happily completing them helped Benny believe in his own future.

Then, finally, Benny needed a sense of equality when caught in moods of extreme anger over actual slights and hurts. He had to face repeatedly the fact that he was capable of hurting others deeply and cruelly, and that sometimes he did it intentionally. That is, he had to beware of being judgmental of others, since he was their equal and would be judged by the same criteria. This was a law of both the Bible (Matt. 7:1–2) and of well-documented clinical psychology. People who are so rigid in their demands on others are invariably hard on themselves. The human subconscious practices an awesome equality in dealing with self and other offenders.

Benny listened often to Jesus' parable of the unmerciful servant (Matt. 18:21–35) and worked at being equally as understanding of others as he wanted them to be with him. Largely on his own insight, he arrived at a surprisingly accurate appraisal of his own self-centeredness. His progress was remarkable.

When the school year was over, Benny still had a long way to go before he would be able to relax around most people. However, he had a vastly better self-understanding, he had learned the discipline of prayer, and he had started acting unselfishly and enjoying it. When he did overcome his moods and fears, he would have superior gifts for understanding legal offenders —a whole segment of the population that most churches and agencies have only begun to deal with. Maybe this was the calling for which he had been so miraculously restored after the awful automobile accident.

Case 20

Albert, chief of medicine at a community hospital, needed to hear an authoritative declaration that he was equal to others. He held a deep-seated impression to the contrary, planted there by a previous authority figure. He could help others, but his own life was a disaster, and he could not seem to help himself.

The proud and fiftyish physician did not formally request therapy. He just happened to stride into his friend's office for a chat, and his friend just happened to be a Christian psychotherapist. Albert was invited into the interview office, where he collapsed on the patient seat with an already noticeable failure in his facade of classic self-confidence. He grinned uncomfortably as he tried to express his problem without actually admitting that it was in fact a problem.

Albert offered a preface that included facts his friend already knew: he was a millionaire; he was a highly respected medical expert; five of his six children were honor students. He paused to explain that even physicians were permitted to miss on one out of six. He went on to mention his hilltop acreage and his capable wife who presided over his lovely home. All of this marked him as a truly remarkable achiever, especially in the light of the fact that he was the only member of his family who had ever even finished college.

He finally squeezed out the fact that notwithstanding all of this, he was very unhappy, and he could not figure out why. He was in fact so depressed that his staff expressed concern.

On the slightest difference of opinion or the tiniest bit of unpleasantness, Albert would withdraw completely, leaving his staff with the uneasy suspicion that Albert was not capable of managing the hospital. He confessed "If I felt better, I could handle that place with ease. I could pour out the energy and really take care of business. But right now, I could hardly care less."

The therapist friend tactfully probed Albert's case still more deeply. Albert revealed that his father had prophesied often that his teenage son Albert would "not amount to anything." One experience had been particularly traumatic. At age thirteen, Albert had come home from junior high school bursting with joy over a first-place ribbon won in a speaking contest. His happiness was boundless until he told his dad. This perpetual intimidator then hurt his son beyond description when he said, "Boy, what are you so excited about? That ain't nothing. You'll never be able to measure arms with your Daddy." His mother had silently failed to reverse the damage. So the wound festered, and this hardworking lad kept on wondering, "When will I ever be able to measure up? What do I have to do to be equal?"

Albert's depressingly low self-esteem continued into adulthood. The current increase to such alarming proportions was probably due to the fact that his father had died recently without ever changing his damaging verdict. He had accepted Al's gifts, but he had staunchly refused to give him any final approval, even as he had failed to help him in any way to get through college or medical school. The professional standing earned by Albert had apparently been designed to impress this all-powerful and obdurate critic, but now they were finally to no avail. All other recognition was devoid of satisfaction, and Albert was desolate.

As the predicament became clear, Albert began to weep, honestly in touch with his real feelings for the first time in many years. Further explorations led him to wonder how he had ever survived against such crushing discouragement. It dawned on him that an uncle had once assured him that he could make it if he tried. Albert was suddenly and painfully aware that he had not been as grateful to him as he ought. Nor had he been at all careful about his treatment of others, sometimes playing the same kind of discouraging god to others that his father had played to him. He needed from his heavenly Father both gracious forgiveness and the divine seal of equality with others.

The usually very dignified doctor was quite relieved to find his good friend and therapist so accepting of his display of emotion. His gratitude was heightened by a lingering sense of not being worthy of this acceptance. Even as he sensed all this, he was already figuring how to act and look normal when he left the office. He still found too much comfort in the knowledge that his therapist friend was the only one who knew the real Albert.

Before he left he was wise enough to realize that he could take further action to help his condition. In due course, Albert adopted a program of affirmations designed to alter his beliefs about God and life and himself. He liked to think of them as a course of study, but they were much more than that. Two key affirmations about God concerned justice and grace or mercy. As Albert faced the cruelty of his father, he had to leave it to God to judge and punish the man, notwithstanding his newly surfaced anger. He also had to face the fact that he, too, was cruel at times. So he and his father and all persons were equal transgressors as well as equal partakers in God's will that they live abundantly. Albert was taught to see the image of God in others and eventually even in himself. He flooded his consciousness with positive affirmations, and he was deeply renewed and helped to grow.

Although Albert did not continue long-term therapy, his staff and family did notice his new, relaxed warmth. He became more active in his church, phasing it in slowly so as not to attract undue attention. He carried in his wallet a card on which he had written all the affirmations most important to him. He saw himself as equal at least to part of the task of becoming whole.

Case 21

Annette's bout with equality deficiency stemmed from a case of proven incompetence. She needed to learn that God's affirmation does not depend on performance.

Stylishly dressed and well manicured, Annette at twenty-eight had a crippling case of depression. It soon manifest itself in the privacy of the office, as she fell apart piece by piece, eyes floating in tears, her nose red and running. She had been fired from a high-paying job for which she had not been qualified. It had been last in a series of fast promotions made possible by attractive appearance and the compensatory hiring of minorities. She had done so well that she had summed up the courage to terminate a bad marriage after efforts to mend it had broken down. Now she was on her own and petrified with fear for herself and her two children.

Annette was born in a barrio bearing the name "Get Out If You Can" in English. She had become pregnant at sixteen and been forced into marriage to save the honor of her close and loving but severely traditional family. She and her husband and daughter had lived at first in a garage. However, Jess's hot-headed pride paid off in hard work. He studied for a more skilled trade, and they soon moved into a comfortable house. A son was born a year after the daughter, and with two children, this teenage couple never had a chance to finish high school or to finish growing up. Her good grades and gifted mind were lost from serious consideration.

Jess used his resources not only to provide for his family but to squander in gambling and mistresses. Annette, true to her upbringing, became the superhuman mother and longsuffering wife who understood her husband's indiscretions. She had succeeded for awhile, but then she began to feel a boiling resentment. To compensate for her husband's unfairness she took some of the money and indulged in her earlier interests of clothing and education.

Annette finished business school and was immediately placed in a good job. Since she caught on quickly, she was soon moved up without the requisite training. Ever more ambitious, she dropped her resume at a less-than-reputable employment agency, which parlayed her good references into a position well over her head. She was hopelessly inadequate for this slot, and it was impossible to keep her on the payroll.

Now all of Annette's old fears about her inferiority came racing to the surface. Her self-esteem plummeted both because of her ethnic group and her status as a woman. Originally influenced by her placement center to want to prove that women were as competent as men, she relapsed under the weight of her background culture, which prized boys far more than girls. Her own family no longer felt close to or supportive of this outspoken, richly clad woman, and her children's other grandparents were even less help. Now on her own and having difficulty getting any kind of job, she was tempted to believe that her culture might be right, after all, about the inferiority of women and of their own ethnic group. She had not yet run out of funds, but she felt hopeless and deeply hurt.

The counselor sensed how anxious and depressed she was and began with the usual techniques of relaxation. He also advised healthier habits in nutrition and rest. If she could accept less ambitious goals and choose viable options, her proven abilities could easily sustain a rewarding existence. The problem was to get her to do this without feeling further defeated and depressed. In other words, she needed self-confidence immediately so she could get a new job before her unemployment insurance ran out. She also needed to grow out of the syndrome that demanded all or nothing.

Together, Annette and the therapist probed the inferiority feelings that she carried at deep levels. Rather than try to throw out all her upbringing and early teachings, they sorted out the helpful affirmations. She agreed that God is good, for instance, and that she had lost part of this faith and become angry at God because it had seemed to her that God let her fail. In fact, she was having trouble shaking off the idea that God had made all women inferior from the start. It became vitally important that she understand and then feel deeply that in Christ there is neither male nor female (Gal. 3:28). Her apt mind was guided to the list of Bible readings on equality discussed earlier, and she was helped to overcome earlier conditioning with worship experiences on cassette.

The sting of failure was removed both by confession of her responsibility for it, and by affirming that God's offer to draw good out of even this was to be claimed equally by all God's children (Rom. 8:28). It was very healing to give up her repressed anger at God and sense the divine presence in worship now that the blocks were removed. It felt good to be close to God in the way she had enjoyed as a child.

To be sure, there would be people who would not recognize her equality, but the answer was not to downgrade herself to match. They had no power to alter her real standing before God, and God's greatest instruments had tended to be denied equality in the sight of the powers that were in charge. Jesus himself had fallen into this category. To keep her spiritual renewal progressing, she joined a new congregation where women were fully recognized. To support herself she accepted a rather good job, fully within her skills. She was once again vivacious without having to try to be more than she was. Seventeen sessions with the therapist had helped considerably, and with all her fresh insights about equality, she wanted to study some more so she could be what she called "not more equal," but "more careful about developing her potential."

The theme and principle of equality has had too little emphasis either in theology or in therapy. The best antidote for the once stereotypical inferiority complex is the affirmation of equality under God. All other strategies for self-confidence and esteem have far greater hope for success when based on this crucial belief. Otherwise, one risks building self-esteem on achievement, an effort destined all too often to fail. Equality is the human side of the doctrine of grace, where persons claim and indeed celebrate their acceptance of each other.

It may be that equality, an idea critical in the founding of this nation, has been seen for the radical threat that it constitutes against all forms of exploitation and oppression. If this is why it is underemphasized, Americans should recognize that the price for opposing it is not limited to risking a breach of the democratic ideal. Underemphasizing equality, in addition, undermines the spiritual and emotional health of the nation. This has been proven by the decline and fall of every civilization and economy that has sought to fix people in unequal categories. Christian proclamation also needs to strengthen its emphasis on equality, for without humility and equality before God one risks a diabolical affrontery, putting oneself in God's place. However, this doctrine does not simply threaten false superiority. The survival of Soul folk under constant siege is great testimony to its powers of healing and support. This same dogged affirmation formed the foundations of this nation.

9. The Uniqueness of Persons: Identity

"Stir up the gift of God which is in thee." (2 Tim. 1:6)

The second essential Soul affirmation about persons is that each is absolutely unique and worthy of respect. Both equality and uniqueness have sweeping doctrinal, psychological, and spiritual significance. Unless this uniqueness be true, freedom is undermined by the possibility that one person or a group of persons could be forced to correspond to some other. Mass production in manufacturing has long since begun eliminating individual craftsmanship, and new technology continues the erosion of places to express personal creativity. Without a recovery of reverence for unrepeatability, our culture could breed more and more robotic repetition, and personhood as we know it could disappear from the face of the earth.

The doctrine of the uniqueness of persons is no more closely observed today than is the American dream of equality. Yet individuality is a crucial part of the American dream, and the national heritage of seeing it in the mind of God still prevails. It is not held as sacrosanct nor articulated as forcefully as it ought to be, but it is still in the Constitution. It is also celebrated in the worlds of art and crafts, where fresh creativity is encouraged. The doctrine is readily associated with successful business tycoons, political leaders, and great scholars. And, of course, individualism is the very creed of the growing conservative block. But among the vast majority of America's rank and file, the mass media attempts to herd people into uniform behavior. Uniqueness troubles the established social order in business and industry, in politics and education, and even in many of the churches, where conformity is the order of the day.

Inherent in this doctrine of the uniqueness of persons is not only the political health of the nation but its emotional and spiritual well-being. This affirmation not only recognizes persons; it requires that they *be* persons. To do this one needs to know who one is, or what identity the Creator has assigned. This is no luxury; though few may have a firm sense of self as unique, all who breathe need it as they need free air. Full life is impossible without the knowledge of who one is and the glad affirmation of that identity.

So here, again, is the same interesting question: how did slaves at the undisputed bottom of the social order ever grasp so powerfully the uniqueness of persons, and how did they manage to practice it in this society? The same answers surface again: Blacks drew on African cultural roots, biblical ideas about how God calls and communicates with people, and the simple need for such a powerful doctrine just to survive under oppression. Vital vehicles of expression of reverence for personhood have to be veiled and subtle in hostile environments, but they are no less real and healing. For instance, the praise of God was and is a powerful avenue of soulful personal expression and fulfillment. So it is less a mystery that more praise arose to God from the Soul folk at the bottom than from anywhere else in American society.

The African evidence for the uniqueness of persons is not as obvious as cultural accumulations from the American experience. However, it was the indispensable starting point without which the rest could not have developed. Such an affirmation as the uniqueness of personhood would surely have died in a closed society except for a powerful source or root system. This was to be found in African proverbs and traditional theology, in divine calls to vocations, in spirit possession, and in traditional renditions of the tales and songs of Africa.

In African traditional belief, souls appear before God and receive their unique character. The Yoruba call it one's "ori"; the

Ashanti call it the "kra." In both cases it means an unchangeable destiny as well as a character or personality. So persons stand in awe before both their own unique soul and that of others. This explains why children seem almost to be worshiped and given free rein. The proverbs about letting children play with fire or climb as they wish respect their right to learn as persons. However, Africans also developed a sophisticated system for socializing Souls from heaven.

African traditional religion has widespread doctrines about how the various subdeities call their devotees to priesthood. Blacksmiths and other craftspeople have their patrons inside the monotheistic bureaucracy. One dare not refuse to obey a divine call, but one also is set apart as unique by the same process. Since a call is frequently signalled by spirit possession, it must be clear that the very willingness of a subdeity to possess or indwell a person sets her or him apart as unique and special. African worship, far from the Protestant notion of proper liturgy, has as its ultimate ideal the spontaneous expression of the possessed Soul. This shows ultimate support and awesome respect for personal uniqueness.

The African oral tradition of the performance of tales and songs also undergirded belief in personal uniqueness. In Africa, stories may be considered serious history, and they are expected to be rendered with meticulous accuracy. But the interest of the audience is focused on how the piece will be given the unique touch of the performer. In other words, standard material of saying and song must be stamped with the personality of the soloist, even while its content must be rigidly accurate.

The African emphasis on personal uniqueness survived in the faith and the common culture of Black America, in the churches and in the wider community. Patterns of the affirmation of uniqueness persist in profusion. A brother or sister in church sings, "This little light of mine, I'm gonna let it shine." In the wider community they sing, "It's your thing." Either place, as a soloist audaciously improvises on the theme, the supporting audience cries, "Sing your song," and everybody is fulfilled vicariously by the one person's breakthrough. Instrumental soloists first master the melody, then improvise fluid jazz on the theme. Preachers number among the artists with their colorful oratory, joining the rest of Black culture in affirming uniqueness.

The most dramatic American evidence of all, however, is the healing and fulfilling phenomenon called *shouting*. It occurs in the same permissive and affirming context as the above examples, but it is free of the demand for knowledge of the base melody or tale. In shouting, the ecstasy of possession by the various African subdeities has been adapted to Christian theology, and the Holy Spirit, third member of the Trinity, is now the Possessor. There can be no more powerful affirmation of selfhood than the knowledge that "my good Lord done come by here and blessed my soul and gone." The cleansing or catharsis and release òf a few moments of sincere, shouting ecstasy has empowered Soul folk to stand almost anything for the rest of the week. People who have been too well educated, and thus too culturally inhibited to join in directly have, again, been blessed vicariously by other people's joy and healing.

Like much of African traditional religion, spirit possession too had biblical parallels. The experience in the Upper Room at Pentecost (Acts 2) is the most outstanding example of spiritual ecstasy. The Bible is full of the calls of God, bestowing unique responsibilities not only on persons but on a whole nation or religion. When the Apostle Paul advised the young minister Timothy to "stir up the gift" in him (2 Timothy 1:6), it was no new or strange idea. The Judeo-Christian faith had known of such calls since the call to Abraham or even earlier. There is a sense in which every believer knows oneself to be a unique creation of God, given a set of gifts that lead to the vocation or the calling intended by God. To find this special work and do it is the most satisfying enterprise open to humankind, regardless of financial rewards.

The problem here, as elsewhere, is that the doctrine of personal uniqueness is either applied on a selective basis or subtly denied in much of American faith and life. In the cases that follow, this need is illustrated and measures are prescribed.

Case 22

Gus had an acute need to know and affirm his uniqueness. He was under a mandate to get help as a part of his two years' probation for a first offense of vandalism and resisting the authority of a police officer. The sentence handed down to this seventeen-year-old also included the requirement that he repay the cost of damages done.

Gus really was unique, the offspring of a Black mother and White father. His mother vacillated between demonstrative love and rigid demands; his father was aloof and intellectual and "hard to get close to." These and other problems with relating to significant persons in his life had triggered serious attacks of asthma.

When Gus turned fifteen, his mother demanded that he get a job like other boys in the neighborhood. She wanted him to be resourceful and independent, but just when he complied, they found it necessary to move to a distant community that was much rougher and poorer. Gus, who had never really clarified his identity, was now more confused than ever.

The racial difference between his parents was a major part of his identity problem. As Gus put it, "Being Black *and* White is like being dead. . . . I'm afraid of the world. I don't really belong *any*where, Black *or* White." So far as he was concerned, "Living is hell." Beneath his despair and depression lay a keen resentment that he, a rather handsome, Latin-looking young man, was considered Black at all. "One drop of Black blood, and you're *all* Black," he complained. Yet he longed for the love of his obviously Black mother.

Out of this strange combination of factors he had developed not only deep depression but anger—smoldering frustration and hostility. He felt that nobody really understood his odd predicament. Worse than that, nobody really cared, since they had never been through it themselves. Gus harbored an unhealthy and uncomfortable sense of uniqueness.

The closest thing Gus found to full acceptance and understanding was among a street gang he had originally joined for safety and protection. Their vandalism served as a form of social protest as well as a quest for excitement, while their name meant protection from harassment by nearby gangs. This bunch was both ethnically mixed and emotionally mixed up, and they found common comfort in their shared alienation and anger. Providentially, Gus's therapist was also racially mixed, and he had early gang experiences similar to Gus's. He was able to build some rapport on this basis; at last Gus had a kindred spirit who understood!

The therapist did not use this similarity to downplay the uniqueness of Gus's situation, but he was living witness that the problems of mixed ancestry lay pretty much in how one looked at it. Gus's prime issue was his and his family's ethnicity. It was not so much that Gus was excluded everywhere; he just did not accept his Blackness. So long as he clung to his father's identity or any part of it, he set himself outside Black circles, and he was dealt with according to his own rules. Blacks were responding to his intended distance when they excluded him from their circles. Yet the Whites with whom he tried to relate knew he was not as White as his father, and they never let him forget it. By not accepting his own somewhat unusual identity, Gus therefore invited misunderstanding.

Jesus taught a clever approach to social positions, which the therapist shared with Gus. People should sit at the back when invited to social affairs. Then if the host wants to honor them, they can make the grand advance to the front. However, if they take it on themselves to grab a front seat of honor, and then a more honored guest arrives, it is really embarrassing to be asked by the host to move to the rear (Luke 14:8–10).

Neither Gus nor the therapist believed it was right, but they had to recognize that there was in fact a set of assignments of rank on America's totem pole of ethnicity. If persons proudly and gladly embraced their position as Black and at the bottom, they were then protected against the embarrassment that Jesus talked about. There was no lower slot to which to get demoted. Furthermore, Blacks of character and talent were constantly exposing the injustice of the arrangement. They were also often invited "up." Jesus' advice was tailor-made for Gus.

The therapist also helped Gus overcome his feeling of powerlessness, the actual basis of his towering rage and anger. Gus came to recognize that he had more power and freedom to act than he had realized, albeit within the reasonable boundaries of his family, his community, his minority identity, and his own emotions. He learned to work off frustrations in disciplined outlets such as sports. Wrestling seemed extremely well suited to his needs. Further, he learned to take the focus off himself, and he returned to gainful employment. He accepted a job negotiated for him in a facility for the mentally retarded, and he surprised himself with his effectiveness in that setting.

The greatest progress, however, could be seen in Gus's new view of himself as unique. While he had previously considered his position between White and Black to be a source of rejection, he now came to see his bicultural status as a relatively unique asset. The biblical model the therapist used was the young man Timothy, whose father had been a Roman citizen and whose mother had been a member of the persecuted minority of Jews. The Apostle Paul's key words of advice were useful to Gus: "Let no man despise thy youth, but be thou an example. . . ." (1 Tim. 4:12) and, "Wherefore I put thee in remembrance that thou stir up the gift of God, which is in thee. . . ." (2 Tim. 1:6). Timothy's mixed parentage gave him access to the best of both cultures: Greco-Roman and Judeo-Christian. He was thus biculturally competent, as had been Paul, and as was Gus! Paul had been the bridge between Jerusalem and Athens, and Gus might also use his bicultural position for great good.

After fifteen sessions with the therapist, the report to Gus's probation office was, "marked improvement." His dependence on the gang had greatly diminished. For the first time in his life Gus embraced his Black identity enough to associate with a largely Black church whose members accepted him unconditionally. This was both healing and enjoyable beyond his fondest expectations, especially since the church included a number of young women.

Since Gus was finishing his high school work, wrestling would have to be continued in the community college. His hostilities were greatly reduced, but he would need such an outlet for some time to come. His work with the mentally retarded was more and more rewarding. In fact, it seemed as if his keen talent for understanding and relating to them might very well be the "gift" he should "stir up." Life was too rewarding to be angry at everyone anymore.

Case 23

Gert, age twenty-eight, was a near basket case of low self-esteem. She had been looking for help when she heard the therapist speak on success before a group of salespeople. Before the speech was half over, she knew help could be found. Her need concerned the opposite of success; what the speaker was saying about the unleashing of each person's powers was the reverse of anything she knew about herself. *"What powers?"*

Gert's need was real. "I am so afraid of failing at everything that my hands *stay* cold and sweaty." She also had chronic headaches and nervousness bordering on panic. Close observation revealed a subtle but perpetual fidget. Her levels of undifferentiated fright sometimes caused attacks of diarrhea.

Her mind was haunted by the specter of helplessness to the extent that she would lose her grip on reality. During such episodes, she was detached from her own senses, perceiving actual experience as a fantasy. In her dreams, which often seemed more real than life, she was unable to care for herself. Still worse, equally catastrophic things rendered those dearest to her helpless as well. Her shaky boundaries between the worlds of fiction and fact only added to her terror.

Gert's life began when her mother endured an exceptionally long period of labor. Her mother never really recovered from it, and she died before Gert had reached age two. Gert's family remembered her as crying constantly when separated from her infirm mother, and she herself recalled hearing early that she had "killed her mother." She had registered a childish, horrified surprise at having perpetrated this innocent evil, and she had spent the rest of her life dreading the possibility of equally grave and unintentional errors on her part.

Thus Gert's life was haunted by the twin specters of massive mistake and utter helplessness. The latter sense was only accentuated when, at age twelve, she was fully restrained after an operation for tonsils and adenoids. She felt so helpless she was sure she would die. Thus she entered her teens desperate for full acceptance and increasingly afraid she would not deserve it because of her failures and helplessness. This motivated high effort and performance on her adult job, winning her a reputation for diligence and strength. Meanwhile, she was quite accurately perceived as sensitive and understanding, and many people poured out their troubles to her willing ears. She helped others, but she could not help herself, and nobody else was trying to assist her.

In fact, none of Gert's relatives or friends were close enough to try. She was far removed from her aging grandparents, who had been largely responsible for rearing her. Nor was she close to her father, who had long since remarried. Gert, who had begun with such unusual needs, was now dangerously self-dependent, in terms of her emotional life. She lived in mortal fear that if she were ever known as she really was, no one would like her. She could not figure out why coworkers were so drawn to her. She voiced a wistful desire to be "free to be me," when in fact she had not the faintest idea who she really was.

Because she was so hungry for help and open to the therapist's style, it was not hard to determine how to treat her. Following the usual preliminaries, they addressed her beliefs about God and herself. She had not been "good enough for God to let her mother live." She herself was a living mistake who could not be trusted even to engage normally in her own birth. Since she assigned to herself all blame for everything bad that had happened since, she could not trust herself to do anything but wrong. Gert had no self-worth; she saw in herself none of the personal dignity that God bestows on every human being.

The therapist tried a method combining her interest in his speech on success with her interest in religious things. He asked her if she thought Jesus was a success at "selling" his program to the world. When she readily responded, "Of course!" he countered with, "If you could become like Jesus, would that help?" Gert was not sure; "Jesus was God and all good." Furthermore, she recalled teachings about him as a sacrificial lamb that the world was "free to slaughter." She summed up this discussion saying, "He had the power to get up from it. It would *kill* me to be any more vulnerable than I am." However, when the therapist quietly repeated his question, she stopped resisting and finally said, tentatively, "Well, it would help to be like Jesus if I could have his power to get up from the beatings the world likes to dish out."

Following this lead, the therapist prescribed a series of mental and spiritual exercises he was developing around the acronym CRAVE. Meditating on "C," she was to focus on the attributes of Christ with which she was to become identified. He was good, and so was she. He went to the cross out of strength, not weakness; her problems had no basis in weakness on her part either. He understood all people, and she was known for this too. He knew all about her, and she could learn to understand herself much better.

"R" was for relaxation of both body and soul. She was to stop judging herself so harshly and accept the verdict of God, the all-wise authority on such matters. She had always been unconditionally accepted in God's gracious sight, and physical relaxation was to be augmented by complete mental calm in the certainty of God's love. Mental and spiritual peace helped the physical relaxation, and when a muscle refused to relax, she would know that it was reflecting some leftover inner tension.

The "A" was for affirmation of herself as the unique person she was born and equipped to be, with all the attributes of Christ in her. She was to practice sensing herself this way during interaction with others, but she was not to mention Christ or brag about her growing likeness to him in any way. To her surprise, there was a marked and almost immediate response to her more positive view of herself. Her fellow employees gave her still more compliments and confided in her as never before. All this was gratifying, but it took a little time to grow comfortable with the compliments, since they contradicted the residue of low self-esteem that still lurked in her depths.

The "V" was for visualization in vivid detail of the person she was now becoming. She was literally to see in her mind the person she was already affirming. This looking was to be disciplined, both in the time spent doing it and in the believability of detail. The picture was to be so convincing that she would see it even when she was not focusing on it. These visions were to be intensified when possible by appropriate religious music. She was to hum the music whenever possible, driving her car or washing the dishes, so that the new Gert would be called to mind.

The final "E" drew attention to her need to experience the abundance of life in Christ. She was to give herself wholly to the flow of new power and insight, rather than simply to talk of the Christian life. This point required the most time in succeeding appointments. Bad emotional habits and the negative core beliefs that go with them do not easily surrender their grip on people. Gert found it helpful to retrace and talk out the circumstances in which she tended to "slump back into the old habits" acquired over many years. At times she needed to summon all her determination to cooperate to keep from giving up.

Gert's recovery process was enjoyable. Visualizing to taped music was often pure joy, and she loved the conferences. She went her way enthusiastic about her unique new identity and her increasingly recognized gifts.

Case 24

Carl's need for identity and self-worth was really crucial; his very livelihood depended on it. As a professional athlete he needed self-confidence to overcome deteriorating performance on the field. Being recently married and expecting a child added to his need for shoring up his performance. The solving of the problem was complicated by the fact that teammates were putting extra pressures on him, because they resented his marrying out of his race. In fact, they seemed at times to prefer that he make a hot-headed mistake rather than a winning play for the team. One sympathetic teammate saw the violent danger signs and suggested that Carl get some help, and Carl took his friend's advice.

Carl's family history revealed that his temper problems grew largely from his underprivileged environment. Most of the children where he grew up formed a lifelong feeling of powerlessness and inferiority. Carl had never been able to consider the world outside his ghetto friendly. Neither the public schools nor the media, his two contacts with that world, had done anything to help the low self-esteem among his group. More often, they had reinforced it. His one escape from frustration had been athletics, and he had practiced relentlessly, making great use of his marvelous physical endowment.

Coaches and owners coveted Carl's strength and speed. He was signed up with a professional team before finishing college. The first two years went well enough, but just when he was reaching his prime, his fellow players turned against him through jealousy. He was marvelous on the field but helpless in the mental tricks played on him by players and coaches alike. When his frustration burst out, as it inevitably did, Carl expressed it in his old street idiom, and he was branded as a not-too-bright troublemaker. He became the butt of more and more jokes, and associates insinuated he was not up to team standards. He was probably kept just to avoid having to face him on an opposing squad.

The easiest answer to Carl's woes would have been to find a new team and coaching staff, one that would free him to do his best and appreciate him for it. With this not likely for the time being, Carl's therapist had to help him find a way to cope with both the bad situation and his own limitations as a person. The mental game plan started with relaxation disciplines and moved on to the critical phase of self-understanding. They then moved on to ways of communicating in a hostile environment, with strategies for action on the field and off.

Increased self-understanding served the purpose of increasing self-esteem. The therapist began the inventory by focusing on Carl's knowledge of life on the street, helping Carl to recognize it as valid, useful wisdom. Carl was able to read people quite accurately, having a penetrating insight into human nature that the therapist frankly declared was superior to the naiveté of the typical middle-class team members. Carl now had to stop getting scared and angry and learn to use his wisdom. He had always known pimps and hustlers who used street wisdom for evil purposes; now he would use it for high principles of fair play. Carl learned that he was equipped with inner strength as well as physical power, and he was intelligent enough not to have to be scared.

With this new self-understanding, he learned to deal differently with his problems. He could now reverse the field and stop being always on the defensive. He learned to listen to the sick jokes and calmly fire back when appropriate. All the old Black culture tricks of "signifying" could be used to good advantage if he stayed cool. Over a period of two seasons, Carl's therapist helped him to see himself as having real advantages; he could think of his background as a kind of good luck. This attitude helped improve Carl's already good game, and his newly articulate confidence helped him emerge as a team leader. Now he would have to be reckoned with: either he would be paid a satisfactory salary and used fairly, or they would have to trade him away. Carl had found the strength of his own identity and he had learned to use it to good advantage. His future was indeed brighter than it had ever been.

The unique identity and worth of the individual is a matter of profound religious and psychological significance. Far more than is commonly acknowledged, individual identity is the very foundation of true moral accountability. Without the individual, there can be no individual responsibility. Yet the mass media and massive social and economic pressures are seeking to regiment people's behavior and thus undermine the very cornerstone of a democratic society. Personal uniqueness and vocation under God are also affirmations of faith, especially in light of the pressures of mass society and the propaganda of the extremist groups that preach hatred and group superiority. The good news of the gospel of Jesus Christ includes for all the love of neighbor as of self.

Indeed the two are impossible to separate. If one is not happy about the person God created, how can one be glad about the Creator? Recent innovations in churches have shown that the need in this area is so great as to deserve whole series of programs and even revivals. People whose spiritual life was dismal despite their serious disciplines report a new joy and productiveness in their devotional life. Because their church seriously focuses on the issue of personal uniqueness and identity, they have found new peace and new power in their practical as well as spiritual lives.

Self-esteem, or affirming the goodness of one's identity, is the other side of the goodness of God and creation. The same sorts of goodness that must be affirmed in creation must be affirmed in unique and specific detail about the self. People will always need to be saved, but emphasizing a term like *wretch* (used in the hymn "Amazing Grace") and thus helping to maintain depression leaves them too far from the kingdom to be able to accept the grace of God when it is offered. Celebrating one's unique identity and gifts is a most healing way of praising God. The psalmist said it well: "I will praise thee; for I am fearfully and wonderfully made: marvelous are thy works; and that my soul knoweth right well" (Ps. 139:16).

10. The Family of God and Humanity

"Have we not all one Father?" (Mal. 2:10)

The third and most visibly pervasive affirmation of Black belief about people is that they are all related as a family. While the majority culture in America sometimes includes a somewhat parallel notion of neighborliness, there is a typical difference in degree if not in kind of relationships. Western society tends to see families as nuclear, each the extension of an individual, each producing a succeeding generation of other individuals. Extended family relatives are a topic for jest and derision. They are stereotypically poor, thus constituting an implied obligation that threatens the stereotypical rich uncle. Clan groupings such as the Rockefellers, DuPonts, or Kennedys appear to be exceptions to the trend, but their familyhood may not be as intimate or as altruistic as that of America's Black masses. In a word, Soul folk treasure kinship in a manner not common in the prevailing lifestyles of this land.

Of course, outbursts of extended family experimentation are fairly common both historically and currently, but they are always countercultural. Groups like the nineteenth-century Oneida Community of New York as well as hippie communes and more recent religious communities have found it impossible to resist both internal and external pressures. From the outside comes disapproval. From the inside come relapses into the rank individualism and acquisitiveness of the wider culture. There simply has not been in mainstream America a vision of family or community that can seriously be compared with ideal lifestyles of Blacks, Native Americans, and other presumably primitive cultural and ethnic groups.

Yet it is widely recognized that the best way to acquire a healthy sense of equality and uniqueness is to grow up in a loving family. The difference is that Soul folk define the family group in much broader terms. The larger vision of humankind as a kinship group influences much of the interaction throughout the traditional Black community. Like the constitutional presumption of innocence until proven guilty, this belief system presumes folk to be related and obligated to each other until proven otherwise. The well-known Western and biblical doctrine of the Church as the family of God is not articulated very much among Blacks, but it is followed seriously in practice. In fact, it spreads in varying degrees of literalness on beyond the churches to the entire Black community. During the depression of the 1930s, White hoboes persistently dropped off their trains to beg food in poor Black neighborhoods, knowing that both good cooking and familial generosity were the rules rather than the exception. The slogan of the ghetto has long been: "We are family!"

On grounds like these no Black should ever be presumed particularly pious just because she or he greets passersby with such churchly titles as "Brother" and "Sister." This vocabulary is as common in the jails and on the hardened streets as it is in churches. It is firmly imbedded in the language and world view of the ghetto; it is an unchallenged image in the frame of reference called Black culture. But again the question arises. "How on earth does so humane and idealistic a view take root and blossom in such unlikely soil?"

The now familiar answer is that African tradition, Bible images and ideas, and the necessities of survival planted and nourished this vision of extended family society. Only an indestructible solidarity based on the need for survival could ever have brought Blacks through the seeming hopelessness of slavery. Welfare workers today see the same kind of closeness and sharing among Blacks as playing havoc with laws necessarily based on the isolated nuclear family idea. If this functional sense of Blacks as one were to die, the survival of the whole race would soon be in jeopardy.

The evidence of cultural roots brought over with captured Africans still everywhere abounds. Titles like "Uncle" and "Aunty" were used by Whites to avoid the presumed dignity of "Mr." and "Mrs.," but these filial appellations were copied from the slaves themselves. They, in turn, were simply doing what they had always done in the villages of the homeland. There the entire population was blood kin, back to the ninth generation. Their vocabulary was so biased in favor of the family that there were no title equivalents for persons as far removed as a "Mister."

The ideal of the family as more than a mere living arrangement has philosophical support from sage African proverbs. "Because we are, I am," say the Akan and Ashanti. This is the direct opposite of glorified individualism. The Yorubas insist that wisdom is impossible without the input of the larger group: another Yoruba proverb declares, "He who has the support of others can achieve great things." This is not lofty idealism; it is the realistic insight of an early type of civilization. African ideals were not Eden-like innocence, a fact clearly seen in the cruelties of wars between groups not considering themselves part of the same family or tribe. However, the kinship group and the deep indoctrination in it were the only way Blacks knew to relate to persons close to them. Thus every woman of childbearing age in any given slave quarter was aunt or mother to all the children in her brood's age set. This exactly parallels the African experience described in the book *Roots*. Kunta Kinte's age set at initiation into puberty were his "brothers," while their mothers were his "mothers" (Haley 1976).

Needless to say, these tribal groups were similar to the "twelve tribes of Israel" in the Bible. In fact, it has often been noticed that the culture of the Old Testament closely resembled that of African traditional religion. The Bible wisdom that "God setteth the solitary in families" (Ps. 68:6) could as easily have been an African proverb. The creation story in Genesis 2 affirms that human beings were not meant to live alone. No Jew can deny kinship to any other, since they all have Abraham for their father, and the Old Testament tradition thus takes relatedness for granted. The same is true in Black culture.

The extended family ideal as such does not receive attention on the typical menu of Black preaching. There seems to be no specific text urging, "Be ye family," and preachers rarely choose Malachi's question, "Have we not all one father?" (Mal. 2:10). The message is proclaimed, however, in other guise: "Bear ye one another's burdens" (Gal. 6:2), or, "Inasmuch as ye did it unto the least of these my brethren [filial title], ye did it unto me" (Matt. 25:40). Furthermore, the Black pulpit clearly fosters the family ideal, urging assistance to the tired and homeless, burying the penniless dead, and feeding the hungry. The organized churches are undeniably the household of the faith and the very literal family of God's people. But the wider community partakes of virtually the same commitment.

Family relatedness is both literal and de facto. Many Black churches in the West and North are composed of an exended blood kin group transplanted from their town of origin in the South. But the mystique of family has a momentum and life all its own. Thus one can depend on finding a family without any blood ties whatever. A recent incident profoundly illustrates this fact. A sleek sedan drew up to a church I pastored in the West and discharged a well-dressed Black woman. She and the white family she served were all new in town, having just moved across the continent. The family left her at the curb with no introductions, knowing that she would shortly acquire an impressive collection of church-family kin. In fact, more people wished to adopt her than was practical. She found a surplus of places to eat and sleep when she was away from her domestic chores. It is ironic that this is exactly what her White employers expected to happen. As apparent experts in the needs of domestic technicians, they knew that such workers simply had to find some kind of participation in a familylike arrangement, especially when they were removed from their blood kin.

Outside the church the vision of kinship is visible in the treatment of two usually very powerless groups, the very young and the very old. Children are seen as the greatest of blessings in a tribal society. In this country, even when the Black believer has almost nothing material with which to care for a child, one finds it impossible to resist taking in a needy one. The legalization of abortion has not greatly affected the number of homeless children, and the Black culture still tends to create "relatives" as needed. Every Black community has a house where grandchildren, nieces, and nephews—blood kin and otherwise —dwell together. It is significant that they live there until they mature, often treasuring the ties for life.

Likewise, the elderly are honored and respected, and far fewer of them live out their last days in warehouselike centers for the aging. These old folks are important as rearers of the children of working parents, and indeed as the authority figures in home and church. In the Black community it is considered a disgrace to have to be cared for in an institution if one has children. Senior citizens' homes sponsored by Black church corporations have been known to fail simply because no one wanted to go there and suffer the stigma of having no family who cared enough to take them in. With American mobility, this pattern is eroding, but the dream and ideal are still alive and well.

Nostalgia for family and community is not unique to the churches. An urban anthropologist named Elliot Liebow found that Black personalities on the street corner romanticize their all-important friendships, preferring to believe or at least act as if these ties reached back into the distant past. They insist on modeling their exchange of necessities on a family basis impossible to maintain amidst their severely limited resources (Liebow 1967, 166–67, 176). This yearning is probably the result of more than cultural momentum or habit. The family mentality has circulated necessities and saved people from starving and going insane, not only in the dim past but recent months and weeks, keeping alive the vision of an extended family society.

It is possible, of course, to take filial oneness too far. For instance, one could be so completely a function or product of the kinship group as to feel trapped in their transgressions and paralyzed by their inertia. This sort of overidentification with the group caused the Prophet Ezekiel to declare to his fellow Hebrews in exile the first real doctrine of personal accountability. His speech went something like this: "Away with this business about fathers eating sour grapes and their children's teeth being set on edge. All souls are mine. As the soul of the father is mine, so also is the soul of the son. And the soul that does the sinning, that's the one that's going to die" (18:2–4). In the intervening years, both Jewish and African cultures have evolved into a more middle ground between group and individual identity. The more moderate position of Black culture resulted from a practical recognition of the usefulness of a view that left room for individuals. However, they remained bound together in a family or community, so they could withstand storms. Without families, individuals in isolation could never have endured hardships.

Moreover, Black cultural roots emphasizing the family are important here for still another reason: they constitute a link of commonality with other less industrialized cultures within North America. The extended family society is alive and well in many Native American communities. Japanese-American funeral corteges extend to record length, indicating that many people take the extended family ties seriously. Other Asians and Hispanics also follow the pattern. All testify with equal insistence that close family relations and unconditional acceptance must be accompanied by serious mutual obligation. The loving care that such a family provides is essential for babies, of course, but it can never really be outgrown in any culture. At most it can only be covered up.

This fact is illustrated in the following cases, even though in two of them the family relationship used to help and heal was not prescribed by a clinical professional. Rather, it was the cultural inclination and traditional common sense and compassion of church folk that rallied the needed support.

Case 25

Sophronia was a classic case of need for a family support system. She was of Italian and Slavic ancestry: her surname from the latter culture was spelled with eleven letters. She had traded it for a much simpler English married name at age nineteen, after almost a year on her own. She then moved with her new husband to his graduate school and resumed her sophomore-level studies at a nearby state university. Both were good scholars; they were a promising couple indeed.

However, Sophy soon found life too complicated for her to perform at her best. She was caring for her tiny household, carrying one and sometimes two part-time jobs, and then trying to attend classes and study. Yet her heroic efforts to keep her household afloat were taken for granted by her husband. He gave her almost no emotional support. In fact, he often made her feel inferior right in the home she labored so hard to maintain. An increasing inward terror paralyzed her mind when she tried to concentrate on her schoolwork.

Little by little Sophy developed the habit of curling up to study on the sofa of her next-door neighbors. Their apartment was as small as her own, but she functioned much better there. The neighboring couple, much older graduate students, did not understand what was going on, but they were permissive and warmly hospitable. This form of openness easily fitted into their former lifestyle in the Black ghetto. In time they came to understand that the natural, unquestioning acceptance they gave this "child" (as they called her) was a necessity denied her everywhere else. In their home she received love not unlike what they bestowed on their own offspring, who were her age and older.

The three people presented a strange spectacle: a young blond woman curled up on the sofa of the Black couple she had appointed to be her surrogate parents. The three studied without a word, but the household radiated a warmth that relaxed and healed overloaded Sophy, who often fell into a gentle sleep.

Eventually Sophy became aware of how much her husband was exploiting her. After one summer vacation she filed for divorce and did not return to school. However, she did not give up her surrogate parents. When her life again became complicated and full of stress, she often gave them a long-distance phone call.

In time Sophy remarried, and she and her husband visited her former place of residence, which was also his home town. They spent a night in the home of her old friends, where they talked for hours after dinner. As Sophy and her husband, a very competent but quiet technician, were about to go to sleep, he aptly summed up what he had seen. "These people seem more like your parents than any of your blood kin or anyone else we have met." He wondered why she had never told him just how much these surrogate parents meant to her. It would certainly have helped explain the phone bill at times.

Her husband's insight caused Sophy to crystallize in hindsight how much her extended family had actually meant to her. Next morning she shared her heightened awareness with the hosts and thanked them profusely and with tears. She now knew that without this special anchor, her periodic therapy and occasional periods of happiness and abundance would not have been enough to keep her whole. She would probably draw on these dear people for the rest of their lives, but she would do so now with awareness and with deep appreciation.

Case 26

Kate was also destitute of a family support system, and she, too, had no accurate name for her need. She was twenty years and her daughter was twenty months old when she shared with her new pastor the fact that she was being treated for what she called a nervous breakdown. It had all started less than two years before, when she had left home as an unwed mother, accepting an invitation to live with a close relative in a distant city. She was allowed to stay free of charge in return for housekeeping and other domestic services. But financial demands increased fairly soon, and Kate tried to hold two jobs, care for her baby, and do chores around the house. When she finally broke under the strain, she was placed on Aid to Dependent Children and advised by her worker to rent her own small house with the money they provided monthly.

Kate saw this house as a real haven, and she kept it spotless. her two-year-old daughter was now cared for all the time by an adoring mother, and all appeared well, except that Kate could not sleep at night. In fact, the medications prescribed only seemed to compound her problems and build her fears. No dosage of tranquilizers could mask her deep anxieties. She began to fear that she would snap and have to be institutionalized. Yer her conversations showed that she was quite rational and firmly determined to be a responsible and effective single parent.

Her pastor finally sensed that his first diagnosis of Kate's problem as unresolved guilt was far from accurate. Considering the rigid background from which she had fled, Kate had a surprisingly good acceptance of herself as an unwed mother. Her more pressing problem was rather loneliness, a perception of herself as utterly isolated and vulnerable. An unidentified threat stalked her small frame. Even with excellent police surveillance, better-than-average care by the welfare department, and, now, a new church anxious to assist in every possible way, Kate sensed herself to be without protection. In the middle of the night she was overcome by nameless terror that seemed to hang within arm's reach. The pastor finally recognized that Kate needed not only acceptance but emotional support—a mother substitute to replace the one she had had in happier years.

The church's membership included another needy person. At age fifty-six, Ella had lost her only child, a son of twenty-nine, in an auto accident. He had lived with his parents and had been unusually close to his mother, who was proud of her ability to bridge the generation gap and relate not only to him but to his many friends. She had lived not only with but through her son. Now he was gone, and despite all the efforts of his friends, she was desolate. It occurred to the pastor that her needs matched Kate's needs, if Ella would accept a daughter rather than a son.

Despite all the pastor's attempts at diplomacy, Ella's first response was a flat declaration that nobody would ever be able to take the place of dear Harry. The pastor persisted. He sympathetically affirmed that no one would ever mean to her what Harry had meant, and he explained that he was simply looking for an old professional in the field of mothering. He was asking her to meet a desperate need for which she had the precise talents. It worked; she accepted. Furthermore, it took only a short while for Ella to evolve into an enthusiastic mother and grandmother. Almost involuntarily she not only called on the phone every morning; she visited regularly, cooked goodies, and bought gifts. They took rides together, went shopping, and had picnics. It was a most fruitful arrangement for all.

Kate soon went off all medical care for her nervous condition. Ella was occupied and delighted, enjoying similar independence from drugs. Ella was quite careful, of course, to keep a piece of her overwhelming grief alive, but she was never even remotely able to live up to her earlier prophecy that she would never again smile. The healing and the pleasure were irresistible.

On one occasion Ella commented rather frankly and gratefully on how surprised she was that her very tall son had in some sense been compensated for by a very short and otherwise different daughter. Kate, Ella, and their pastor agreed that all people are designed by God to fit into families. Whoever tries to survive without some sort of deep, familylike relationship is being too self-demanding.

Case 27

Shelly's history showed a gradual loss of all significant family ties for reasons over which she had no control. Her needs became critical when her marriage ended. Shelly and Joe, both twenty-eight, had been promising professionals, each with an attractive appointment in a major corporation. They had also been studying for graduate degrees in their spare time and struggling to buy a home. Then quite suddenly it all went sour. The marriage ended in separation and divorce, and Shelly now lived alone in an almost empty apartment.

Within the previous five years Shelly had lost both of her parents. Since they had been estranged for years, Shelly had had to help her mother with the younger siblings. She had thus worked extremely hard at home and on jobs to earn her way through college. In all of these stressful situations she had seemed virtually indestructible. Now she was at the end of her rope.

Through tremendous effort, Shelly was keeping a pleasant face on her job, but she would go home and cry, sometimes for hours. This, combined with sleeplessness, poor appetite, and severe loss of weight, motivated Shelly to seek help. She approached the counselor at her church's pastoral counseling service.

The counselor expressed admiration for her long history of unselfish service and devotion. He suggested that one of her problems might be that she was for the first time in her life completely detached from loved ones. Her younger brothers and sisters had all moved far away. Without parents, siblings, or a spouse, she had no one on whom to bestow her usual self-giving. The answer was a surrogate family. Shelly was reticent at first, but she readily agreed when she found that it did not necessarily mean moving in with them.

The counselor determined that the Washingtons would be an ideal couple to ask to adopt Shelly. They were warmly personal retirees, living interesting lives and enjoying each other and their spiritual family to the fullest. At first they too were hesitant to take on the obligation of another godchild. They had plenty already. The counselor corrected this impression by suggesting that this assignment might resemble Peter's ministry in which he said, "Silver and gold have I none, but such as I have give I unto thee (Acts 3:6). They tentatively accepted the proposal.

The rest went unusually well. The Washingtons had never had a daughter as mature or as grateful as Shelly. She cared for them with unaccustomed niceties, treating them to evenings out for dinner and an occasional concert. The Washingtons reciprocated with the originally recommended daily phone calls. Shelly still lived alone, but she was watched over and cared for constantly. For all concerned, the rewards far exceeded their expectations.

Today, Shelly and her loved and loving parents are pondering how their church and all churches might minister more effectively by enlarging the family mode of ministry that has meant so much to them. They are sure that the same plan could be used to heal thousands and provide abundant spiritual and other joys.

The authors searched far and wide for illustrative cases involving men, but they found no comparable instances of successful surrogate family assignments for male clients. This was obviously no accident; it deserved examination. They determined that the answers fell into two categories: male incidence of seeking or not seeking help, and the clinical evidence of male need.

It has been well established that women far exceed men in their willingness to seek help with emotional problems. This in itself does not necessarily mean that men are either more or less emotionally healthy than women. It simply means that men try to live independently out of an acquired image of male self-sufficiency. They falsely perceive that seeking help is a sign of weakness. It is also true that men are not as powerless and as frequently crushed as women. Powerlessness figures more prominently in women's requests for help. The dearth of instances where men have been assigned to a surrogate family may be largely due to the fact that so few seek assistance of any kind when they have emotional problems. It may also be that they typically refuse to recognize even so fundamental a need as the need for an emotional support system.

The clinical evidence surely suggests that men are far too human and vulnerable, however, to survive without a functioning family. E. M. Pattison and M. L. Pattison of the Medical College of Georgia have indicated that all persons are mentally and emotionally healthy in proportion to the size of their system of supports (1981, 136). The fact that men do not formally seek supports only means that they often devise less obvious ways to meet their needs. Black communities abound with spontaneous parenthoods supposedly honoring the elderly. Few of them fully recognize the value they have for the adopted children. Even when it is faced, it is far less likely to connote weakness. Such filial ways are "the very will of God!"

One of the authors and his wife serve as dean and program director in a predominantly male and Black seminary. They unabashedly espouse the uncommon model of the academic community as a family. Their counseling thus sometimes evolves toward parenting. Direct use of titles like "Mom" in private conversation may seem to undermine the respect due a professor, but it serves the goals of education. While on the one hand it appears to place an unbearable burden on faculty as surrogate parents, on the other it makes easier their task of reaching deep need. The best scholarship demands a healthy psyche.

In academia as everywhere else, the family is an indispensable part of survival and health. It is far less of a mystery how Blacks have survived when one ponders the power of this Soul affirmation of humanity as the extended family of one parent. If the wider society is to avoid disintegration, this principle must be accepted and implemented among all peoples. We must have a means of bonding persons beyond the nuclear family, whether in church or elsewhere. No matter how mobile the nuclear family, and regardless of the absence of blood kinship, persons must be deeply and warmly related. The culture of the powerless Appalachians, Native Americans, and Blacks must in a sense become normative for all, so that the better aspects of American civilization may survive and thrive.

11. The Perseverance of Persons

"And let us not be weary in well doing: for in due season we shall reap, if we faint not" (Gal. 6:9).

The Soul system's fourth and concluding affirmation about persons is that they can and should endure or persevere in their identity and faith. People do not have to surrender to the pressures of life and give up in despair. If there is one test to which every system of belief should be subjected, it is this: the test of its ability to sustain and empower believers and to help them cope with life. No degree of orthodoxy can compensate for deficiency in this aspect. The final proof of the validity of the Black folk tradition's view of God and humanity should be sought not in its abstract coherence, but in its ability to uphold and sustain its believers, both Blacks and Whites. All previously treated doctrines such as the Providence of God and the uniqueness of persons find ultimate validation in the way believers handle the stresses of life.

"The perseverance of the saints" is a phrase from the Calvinism of the early American Puritans, a body of belief that included predestination. Some persons were considered to be elected by God to be saved, while others were to be ultimately lost. The elect or saved were called "saints," and they were fully guaranteed to remain saved and persevere in the faith to the end. Their determination to hold out in trust was not just made possible by God's grace; this perseverance was made inevitable by the transforming power of that grace. They had "eternal security," to use another common name for the doctrine.

Ever since the first Great Awakening (a series of revivals in the mid-1700s), many Americans have found this idea of predestination quite repugnant. They have proclaimed heaven as open to "whosoever will" (Rev. 22:17), and they have emphasized the need to choose faith and to stand firmly in it. The strongest and most telling testimony against predestination is the word of Jesus: "Even so it is not the will of your Father which is in heaven, that one of these little ones should perish" (Matt. 18:14).

Standing firm or persevering can easily be taken to extremes also. At times, this heroic effort has resembled that of Sisyphus, the mythological Greek hero, whose glory lay solely in his refusal to give up. Neither perseverance by one's own effort (often called Arminianism) nor the perseverance guaranteed by God (Calvinism) is without serious theoretical and practical problems. If final acceptance with God depends on receiving salvation by faith and then persevering, we are forced to trust our own works too much. If on the other hand there is nothing we can do about being elected to persevere, we are saved or lost regardless of personal effort. Neither is satisfactory in its classical Western expression.

Blacks, with an African-based belief system, have tended to emphasize the positive world view of Gen. 1:26–31 (the goodness of creation), in preference to much later elaborations based on Gen. 3:14–24 (the fallenness of Adam). The African mind knew no total depravity of humanity and so had no need for an abstraction like eternal security to set over against it. For them, life's struggles were real, and its end still unknown, so they trusted the grace of God implicitly. Spirituals therefore declared the need to "Keep yo' hand on the plough, [and] hold on!" It was also necessary to "Cheer the weary traveler, along the heavenly way" and to engage in mutual encouragement and assistance. In other words, the questions about how one would finish life were serious enough to keep one careful, but not so awesome as to necessitate an arbitrarily predestined personal end. The very goodness of God and life was in part due to the interesting challenge provided in the exercise of free will and the power to express one's personhood in decisive acts. Slaves appreciated the healthy uncertainty of life, and they sang, "I wouldn't take nuthin' for my journey now."

Traditional Blacks have rarely debated the merits of eternal security versus human effort. Taking elements from both positions, they lived with little despair and a high dependence on God's grace. A clever paradox perhaps describes their cultural outlook: "Work as if the ultimate responsibility for your salvation depends on you, and trust as if it is all in God's hands." Soul sisters and brothers knew that "the devil can't do me no harm," because they were in God's care. They couldn't be "plucked from the hand of the Lord," (John 10:28, a major text supporting Calvinistic perseverance), but they knew they had to "Keep inchin' along, like a ol' inchworm" in preparation for when "Jesus is coming by and by." However, no matter how conditional these efforts might have been, it never cast any doubt on their expectation to take full part in the "great gittin' up mornin'" or that "great day."

We ask again the haunting question of how so beautiful and functional a faith could emerge from such hard circumstances. As before, the answer continues to be that slaves had to have it to survive. They developed this much-needed stance of trust out of their own cultural roots and biblical sources. Indeed, God so providentially led their development that they produced spontaneously a living synthesis of the best in both Western traditions. Yet they had not the slightest idea that they were creating and testing a folk-construct of profound and lasting theological significance.

It is an interesting irony that the best-known folk tale for teaching all young Americans to persevere is in fact an African story. "The Tortoise and the Hare" is ascribed to Aesop, an African exslave on the staff of the rich King Croesus of Lydia. He rose to prominence as teacher, philosopher, and diplomat on the basis of animal tales brought with him from Africa. The same genre of African narrative wisdom is found in America in the tales of Uncle Remus, the composite, tale-telling exslave, recorded by Joel Chandler Harris in *Uncle Remus His Songs and His Sayings*. These African fables are functional and valuable in any culture, interpreting human experience as well today as they did in the courts of Greece and Asia Minor six centuries before Christ.

Africans used the tortoise to teach patience and perseverance, attributes highly valued in African tradition. A Yoruba proverb declares, "The snail climbs the tree carefully and slowly." This typically low-key statement symbolizes a whole body of wisdom about being watchful, slow, and steady. The tradition teaches firmly that steadiness succeeds where quickness often fails. The Ashanti would assent, using an even greater understatement in proverb: "The tortoise says, 'Haste is a good thing and deliberation is also a good thing.' " The culture of Black Africa breathes caution as opposed to impetuousness and constantly encourages the virtue of patient perseverance.

The culture of the slave era is saturated even more with perseverance. Many American Blacks quote, even today, the old saying: "The race is not to the swift nor the strong, but to him that endureth to the end." The saying is commonly assumed to come from the Bible, but it nowhere appears in that form. The first part comes from Eccles. 9:11 and the latter from Matt. 24:13. Black American oral tradition integrates many Bible passages into its lore. Indeed, to try to separate cultural evidences such as spirituals and gospel songs from the biblical sources is well nigh impossible. The theme of perseverance is too popular to allow record here of all the well-known examples available.

To the spirituals already quoted must be added at least the following: "Done paid my vow to the Lord, and I never will turn back, O, I will go, I shall go, to see what the end will be" (Ps. 116:14 and numerous other Psalms). "I shall not, I shall not be moved, Just like a tree, planted by the waters" (Ps. 1:3). "Walk together children, don't you get weary; There's a great camp meetin' in the Promised Land" (Gal. 6:9). R. Nathaniel

Dett has immortalized in anthem form the spiritual that asserts, "I'll never turn back no more, no more. . . ." And the triumphant note in this last example says it all: "O Lord, I don't feel no ways tired, O glory hallelujah!"

The modern gospel song tradition among Blacks is no less adamant about a typical determination to persevere. A few very popular phrases out of this repertoire illustrate the dominant theme: "I'll let nothing separate me from his love." "I have decided to follow Jesus; No turning back, no turning back." "I promised the Lord that I would hold out. . . Until he meet me in Galilee."

All the way, all the way, I'll be willing, Lord, to run all the way.
If I falter whilst I'm tryin', don't be angry, let me stay.
I'll be willing, Lord, to run all the way.

The corpus of most commonly sung hymns from all sources is no less prone to echo the theme of perseverance. The classic "A Charge to Keep I Have" (Charles Wesley) ends with the fully acceptable warning that "if I my trust betray, I shall forever die." The later hymn by Johnson Oatman, "Higher Ground," provides Black determination with a fitting affirmation: "My heart has no desire to stay where doubts arise and fears dismay. . . . My prayer, my aim is higher ground." Black congregations sing seriously, "The consecrated cross I'll bear till death shall set me free," and, "Sure I must fight if I would reign—Increase my courage, Lord! I'll bear the toil, endure the pain, supported by Thy Word" (Thomas Shepherd).

What may very well be the most poignant and precise of all expressions of Black perseverance was written around the turn of the century by the pastor of a Black United Methodist church, Charles A. Tindley. The chorus reads,

I'm going through, yes, I'm going through;
I'll pay the price, whatever others do;
I'll take the way with the Lord's despised few.
I've started with Jesus, and I'm going through.

The phrases of Black church prayer and testimony by laity are also full of the determination to hold faith: "Pray for me, that I may hold out to the end." "I promised the Lord if he'd change my name, I'd go all the way." "My heart is fixed; my mind is made up." "Now Lord, when this old world can afford me a home no longer, I want to hear your welcome voice saying 'Well done, well done!' "

These pious sincerities have their street-culture parallels, as do all of the major themes of Black belief. One hears the greeting publicized by the Baptist preacher and congressman Adam Clayton Powell, Jr.: "Keep the faith, baby!" And there are the universally used sayings such as, "Hang in there!" and "Keep a stiff upper lip!" or "Keep your chin up!" In the ever-present athletic competitions, teammates keep each other going with, "The game isn't over till the last man is out" or "Go for it!" The Black community's very survival has long depended on the courageous refusal of all to give up or quit on life.

This determination may be distinguished from typical Western notions of perseverance by the fact that it has no ultimate sense of winning over others. Like the race figure in 2 Tim. 4:8, there is a crown or prize in every lane, just for the finishing. Majority culture has sayings such as, "Winners never quit, and quitters never win." But victory in the Soul community has nothing to do with defeating someone else; its sole goal is to survive intact. The commitment not to quit is not against anybody; it opposes only those who would hurt and oppress. Even then, the grim insistence is against only the goals of the would-be oppressor and not against the person as such.

The very utterance of the commitment to persevere is a reward in itself, as well as a kind of self-fulfilling prophecy. With or without conscious use of theological explanations, it serves human needs, nourishing character and strengthening the will. The joy easily detected in the spirituals cited suggests more than a moralistic commitment; it is the celebration of the blessedness born of a firm grip on identity and the ability to express the self with enduring purpose. Perseverance is no mere effort or campaign; it is the continuation of one's highest quest, regardless of opposition, in the faith and hope that one is providently guided, cared for, and guaranteed fulfillment, here or hereafter. One does not get discouraged for long, or try to place a time limit on God's help. Nor does one threaten to leave the will of God if hardships last "just one day longer." Soul folk have taken the "perseverance of the saints" and made of it a vehicle of personhood, an expression of their being, retaining a sufficient amount of providence to keep from being easily frightened.

Case 28

When Harvey, age twenty-nine, came to the clinic, he complained, "I can't seem to follow through on anything. If this keeps up, I might as well give up." A professional football player plagued by loneliness and severe depression, Harvey had been taking marijuana and cocaine, and it was starting to interfere with his game. This resulted in a loss of bargaining power, and he was losing his ability to deal with contracts at all. As his emotions soared and plummeted like a roller coaster, he escaped reality and the task of taking responsibility for himself. A small hint from his roommate was all it took to get him to break his escape pattern long enough to visit the clinic.

His complaints poured out easily. "I lie and escape responsibility." He even realized he was angry at his mother for deserting him by dying in an auto accident. He had considered killing himself, but he could not follow through on that either, especially since his mother would not have been pleased with him. Since he felt unable to stop life, he decided to change his way of living.

His case history revealed that his father left him and his mother when Harvey was only four. His mother had worked hard to support him, and he was unusually grateful. Meanwhile, she had also been atypically sensitive and permissive about her precious only child's ambitions to excel in such rough and dangerous sports as football. Instead of smothering him with overprotection, she had joined him in athletic enthusiasm. It all paid off when he made the professional ranks at age twenty-three. He was soon able to support her in leisure. She was delighted, of course, but no more so than he. They became inseparable. "We were like one person. We were really close. I think I died when she died. I have no desire to go on without her. I can never live life to the fullest without Mother."

Emotionally speaking, Harvey was still an infant locked in the body of a physical giant. In his most lucid and trusting moments, he confessed needs of what can best be expressed as cuddling in his mother's arms. The women he liked were prone to be well endowed like his mother, even though he called them "girls." He was convinced that none of them was "woman enough to replace Mom." All 240 pounds of this giant belonged to a mother whom he refused to allow to die. He had to keep her because of the self-imposed limit he had placed on what he could expect and accept from other women. He had already stopped the clock of his emotional life prior to his mother's death. He was still her husband/protector and her gladiator/son.

However, this fantasy role was not stable. At one moment he would be, as he said, angry at his mother for abandoning him. Then he would feel guilty and do things that the therapist recognized as self-punishment. Depressions associated with his guilt were attempts to share the death state with his mother. They also served the purpose of checking the anger he himself could sense as dangerous. In a way, he had already accepted death for himself rather than to try to control himself and live without his mother.

The therapy prescribed for Harvey moved through five aspects. First, he was helped to bring out and understand and finally to handle his feelings of stress. This helped him to deal with them without the use of drugs or escapes into fantasy. Then he was helped to sort out his own identity, as over against his previous symbiotic existence with his mother.

Thirdly, he was given mental and behavioral exercises affirming the newborn person he was becoming, and he was helped to visualize his new, emerging identity. Then finally, using the discipline and perseverance associated with football practice, he was able to maintain determination to apply all this to handling real life.

Harvey's response to this process was as stormy as his unstable emotional life. Every time he began to accept his mother's death, he would displace his anger onto the therapist. Then he would return to reality, feel guilty, and escape facing the therapist at the next appointment. Later on, as he made real progress, he would fear to go further and miss appointments. He was not anxious to grow up, because he was not at all sure that he could handle that level of mature responsibility.

The therapist recorded a tape for Harvey and instructed him to listen to it on a regular basis. It contained some of his mother's favorite religious songs, and they supported the growth he needed with familiar phrases that reached deep into his psyche. For instance, the song "Precious Lord, Take My Hand" affirmed Harvey's present dependency, but it moved on to say "let me *stand*," which spoke right to his area of need. Another song prayed, "Lord, Help Me to Hold Out." It said what he wanted to say and strengthened his determination, without his having to put it in his own pious-sounding words. This was important, because he was afraid to look or sound as deeply religious as he was becoming.

Harvey had not earlier been able to reduce his dependence on drugs, but he now found that mental and spiritual training were very effective aids in reducing even his desire for drugs. As he concluded his sessions, he knew that his mother would have been proud of the way he was progressing on the drugs and his new tastes in music and reading materials.

Case 29

Patricia's physician, sensing potential suicide, sent her to the clinic. Her eating and smoking habits were already suicidal, and she knew this but had no control over it. She was also chronically guilty, having been upset for four years about failing to visit a friend before she died. All these struggles were quite exhausting, and she was very, very tired and near to giving up.

Pat's life had been discouraging from the very start. Her rigid and sadistic father regularly whipped the children harshly. "You could neither plea nor flee; whatever you did was wrong. In the end, you would lose anyway." Even her menstrual flow gained a negative meaning, after it burst into her life with no preparation. Her father said it was the curse on women due to Eve's tempting of Adam. Her passive mother only made things worse with, "It's a curse all right, but not nearly as bad as the sequel, childbirth." She warned Pat to avoid both sex and children.

Naturally interested in sex, Pat was discovered masturbating at age thirteen, and her parents pronounced her hopeless and incorrigible. To legitimate her drives and overpower her evil self-image, she married as soon as possible at the age of eighteen. When an early pregnancy aborted naturally, she decided it was good, since she was admittedly too evil to be a mother. The marriage soon dissolved also.

Patricia spent the next twenty years trying to become a "better woman" and feeling that she repeatedly failed. Her one stable support was her civil service job, which was structured so as to require no initiative on her part. Away from this basically unrewarding task, she barely existed, eating and smoking too much and struggling with the sin of sex more in her mind than in any actual temptation. It was all very exhausting, nonetheless. She was ready to give up if therapy did not soon succeed in helping her.

Like most obsessive-compulsive personalities, Pat suffered from chronic depression and was habitually self-sacrificing, overly conscientious, and hopelessly perfectionist. She desperately needed approval, and she sought it unconsciously with her extreme helpfulness. Yet she complained at the weight of all these demands. In fact, she was angry at God for letting her suffer so long. In studied detachment, she said, "God is only interested in punishing me. Trusting in him is like dealing with my Pop. Who needs it?" She had good reason to be angry at such a Deity, and her childhood clearly explained whey she had such an idea about God. Yet much of her self-punishing behavior looked very much like attempts to beat the very wrath of God. Her legalistic and dualistic mind kept her forever fearing the opinion of God and a generalized category called "good people."

Following analysis and the typical relaxation disciplines, her therapy focused on creating a new self-understanding. She developed sympathy for the battered child she saw for the first time, but she also needed the authority of the Bible itself to overcome her hard judgments on herself. Bad emotional habits are not easily surrendered, but her compulsive compensations for imaginary sins slowly yielded to the carefully selected good news of the Bible.

Her judgmental father image was replaced with, "Like as a father pitieth his children, so the Lord pitieth them that fear him. For he knoweth our frame. He remembereth that we are dust" (Ps. 103:13–14). This met her mood, and it was coupled with the assurance of pardon in 1 John 1, which ends with the promise to "cleanse us from all unrighteousness" (1:9). She liked what Jesus told the woman in John 8: "Neither do I condemn thee: go, and sin no more." Best of all, it was Mary Magdalene, a woman with an undeservedly questionable reputation, who had the honor of announcing the resurrection (Mt. 28:1–8). God had brought these women to good ends and was working for her good also (Rom. 8:28).

At first, she had trouble believing all those good things were actually there. However, her deep desire to please extended to the therapist, so she worked hard and long at her homework. The new Pat gained enough determination, hope, and personal spiritual momentum that when her twenty-nine sessions were over, she was sure she could keep going.

There would be setbacks, and there was much more learning and growing to do, but with such solid encouragement from the very Word of God, Pat said, "I believe I can make it. At least I know what to do until I do."

Case 30

The Reverend Paul was in town for a national conference when a minister he knew sensed in this usually jovial associate an undercurrent of depression. On the pretext of showing him what a Christian therapist was doing, he lured Paul to the clinic. Examining the therapist's procedures, Paul saw enough of his own need to ask for help then and there. His return home was rescheduled two days later, and he was given an intensive week of analysis and therapy. Daily sessions started immediately; the instant rapport established boded well for the otherwise unfortunately short course.

Since the therapist dared not proceed from an obvious assumption of major illness, and there were no striking symptoms, the analysis was difficult at the outset. Paul was doing the work of two or three busy people and carrying a crippling load of guilt from some relatively minor indiscretions that he reported as major sins. Mental detective work uncovered a low self-image and a fear that people might find out who he really was. The therapist perceived he was trying to break all records and die in a blaze of glory before his true identity was discovered. Paul would thus be protected against the failure he feared at deepest levels.

The therapist broke the news of the unconscious death wish by referring to the prophet Elijah, who also had a great career and yet felt lonely and depressed, openly asking God to take away his life (1 Kings 19:4). The limited time frame required a more than usually directed approach, and the pastor's condition and attitude made it more than usually effective:

1) His increased understanding and acceptance of himself

were to be used to motivate a break with his self-destructive habits of heavy cigarette use and irregular eating of poor choices of foods.

2) He was to get his body in balance with disciplined rest, exercise, eating, and scheduling of work time.

3) Above all, he was to continue the selected reading and listening discipline and the spiritual growth that went with it, so that he could contemplate with seriousness and joy a career of twenty or more years of modestly successful ministry. He need not dread a failure or "be weary in well doing." In due season he would reap the results if he was patient and persevered (Gal. 6:9). God was gracious and provident; he would help Paul on the long-term commitment for his and the people's sake.

4) Pastor Paul was to return for follow-up treatment as soon and as often as possible, unless he was willing to be referred to a local therapist, and provided one of like faith could be found.

As Paul left, he and his new therapist envisioned the day when he would sing with sincerity Clarence Cobb's gospel song: "My soul looked back and wondered how I got over." It might have been entirely different had he not been guided to the clinic in the first place.

The traditions of how to interpret and apply concepts of perseverance are widely varied. They run from a predestined certitude prone at times to breed arrogance, to a compulsive human initiative prone at times to breed depression. Between the two lies the Afro-American tradition of perseverance, which skims the cream off both extremes and nourishes the persistence without which persons lose their very being.

It is preposterous to tell human beings in despair that they may or may not be elected to better things. But it is equally unwise to cry to them that impossible cliche, "Only believe!" If people received support and the right love and encouragement, they would be more likely to believe. Meanwhile, most people wish they could believe and persist with hope and faith. It is the task of ministering people to supply all possible encouragement, in order that real faith may be freely chosen and expressed in real-life perseverance.

12. Some Serious Implications

The most significant implication of this entire effort now becomes clear: people keep or lose healthy emotional balance according to the adequacy or weakness of their *core belief systems*. Whether inside or outside the formally gathered churches, people's deepest belief about God will usually heavily influence if not outright determine their mental illness or well-being. Some core beliefs help people survive and cope, in the deep and abiding faith that God is good and life will always turn out right, no matter how terrible it may seem at a given time. Other core beliefs confer no such competence, so the believer (or disbeliever, more accurately) finds it impossible to persevere and thus gives up. Emotionally balanced persons depend on the Providence of God, holding therefore that life is always worth living. The goodness of God and life will always be disclosed if one will trust enough to wait.

This core belief in light at the end of the tunnel is not necessarily part of the faith of every official Christian. Nor do persons outside the church necessarily lack this faith. The simple fact is that those who do have this basically positive world view can manage to cope with the complexities of life, and those without it often do not.

This idea has compelling implications for a variety of disciplines and interests: people concerned with culture, therapists and theologians, pastors and parents, others in ministry, and members of minorities. It has been a surprisingly provocative pilgrimage for the authors themselves, who held no vision of the abundant implications when the task was originally undertaken. At that time, the work was seen in largely theological and therapeutic terms. The implications developed in more than four years fall into the categories of culture, therapy, theology, ministry, and the family.

Concerning Culture

This collection of experiences suggests a radically revised set of basic attitudes towards spontaneous (sometimes called indigenous) culture and world view. While this approach may seem strange or even threatening to established types of scholarship, it is in fact merely a newly respectful and functional evaluation of the survival kit used by millions of Black Americans. Although this work has focused on that particular world view, other cultures hold similarly supportive systems of belief. In fact, the world has far more territory where so-called "primitive" structure and content prevail in common culture than it has highly industrialized societies. What appears to be new in this approach is novel only in the sense that a folk tradition has been examined for its supportive role in theology and therapy.

One of today's best-sellers perfectly illustrates this point. Lee Iacocca, in his autobiography, frequently refers to his father's philosophy and "homilies." This homespun belief system seems to have provided the strength necessary to tide him over some very difficult times, and the author does not hesitate to say so. The foundational quote clearly expresses a positive world view, or the doctrine of the goodness of God and life: "Just wait, the sun's gonna come out. It always does" (1984, 10). Iacocca said that his father "never let any of us surrender to despair, and I confess that there was more than one moment in 1981 when I felt ready to throw in the towel. I kept my sanity in those days by recalling his favorite saying: 'It looks bad right now, but remember, this too shall pass' " (1984, 10). Iacocca's wife, Mary, reinforced his father's world view, saying at his darkest moment, "The Lord makes everything turn out for the best" (1984, 286). What a productive core belief!

Not every corporation president has had such a father and wife, or such experience of minority oppression. Thus, for some, Iacocca's words might sound like a paean of praise for past patterns of authority. However, recommending the theology of folk culture does not equal an indiscriminate reversal of the clock; this is no anti-intellectual nostalgia. The tenets of seemingly primitive faith are *clinically* tested and in no sense designed to try to undo the Enlightenment or reverse the Renaissance. Rather, our purpose is to recover the healing belief that was thrown out along with medieval religious superstition or overly blind faith. A dear price was and is being paid for the loss of powerful affirmations once clearly believed in spite of ecclesiastical manipulations and misconceptions. So this is an effort in Black theology to conserve a tradition being rapidly lost, while helping the whole of humanity recover a belief system sorely needed.

Again, this revisitation of the simple, healing world view is not to be seen as an unreal expectation violating the intellectual integrity of the modern mind. There have always been some very sophisticated therapists as well as theologians who have synthesized a simple Christian faith with the highest principles of research and practice. Everyone begins from certain assumptions; nobody starts from zero. The traditional Christian starting affirmations pass the test of providing an adequate foundation for life. Meanwhile, the spiritual hunger of the most scholarly can no longer be hidden. The arrogant unbeliever so prominent on campus a half-century ago is far less evident today. Belief systems are more and more an idea whose time has come back.

The popularity of simple affirmations in the widespread flourishing of churches and media ministries emphasizes this point. Although many popular affirmations tend to be terribly oversimplified, their very errors seem to breed growth. The staid, mainline denominations are shrinking year after year, while the "just plain believers" are expanding rapidly. They appeal to this very real need for a substantive belief base from which to begin living. In other words, the declining groups are those who have distanced themselves most from the enormously important national culture, faith base, and worship of the two Great Awakenings. However, the present strength of evangelical faith is more than mere religious nostalgia; the human need for such faith persists, as the cases presented here clearly suggest. The faith that generated the country's highest values is in fact still needed if the nation is to survive in spiritual and emotional health.

To be sure, the first Great Awakening featured some grim views of human nature and some gruesome notions about an angry God who arbitrarily selected some people for eternal fires. However, mixed in with these misconceptions were powerful affirmations like the Omnipotence, sovereignty, and Providence of God. These life-supporting beliefs were built into the everyday culture, and to throw them away with the extremes is to stand in grave danger. Thus the best residue of the Great Awakenings will resurge periodically, if not under more respectable auspices, then by any means necessary. The Providence, justice, omniscience, and Omnipotence of God are essential to the abundant life. Human need will not let them die altogether. At this point one cannot avoid sensing a very deep kinship between Soul culture and the majority's undercurrent of Great Awakenings faith.

Embracing a positive world view does not necessarily imply a complete reversal of the earlier negative views of human nature, however. One sees too many patients in the clinic who have been brutally and deeply hurt to be able to embrace the opposite and naive notion that people are all good. Nevertheless, one can bear the abuse and recover from it when one is fully convinced of the Providence of God. This conviction includes the certainty that nothing too hard to bear will be permitted by God to befall the believer. It is best learned from the cradle on, absorbed from the very atmosphere in a culture of believers. The existence of evil deeds and evildoers makes mandatory a belief in the Providence of God.

Learned minds tend not to think of culture in this role, nor do serious Christians dare suspect that persons can absorb salvation via culture, without personal decision. But the issue here is one of coping with stress and staying whole emotionally and spiritually, whatever that may mean apart from ultimate admission to heaven.

Concerning Therapy

The capacity to cope and remain whole despite great stress directly depends on one's core belief system. A patient's likelihood of being healed is far more dependent on her or his internal resources than on the expertise of the therapist. Although described in a different set of terms, Eugene T. Gendlin's research at the University of Chicago supports this same point. He found that "the successful patient . . . can be picked out fairly easily. . . ." and that "differences in methods of therapy mean surprisingly little" (Gendlin 1981, 3). He has successfully taught people to focus on their inner resources or what he calls "body wisdom." This is no doubt quite comparable to what is referred to as the right hemisphere of the brain, or the intuitive sector of consciousness. This pool of wisdom has not been processed rationally, but it includes the highest insights of humankind, their affirmations of faith. It is here referred to as core belief.

People with adequate "body wisdom" or intuitive levels of trust seldom if ever need therapy for stress. With empowerment of clients as a goal, all analysis of cases mentioned here involved examination of belief systems, and all therapy included serious and basic effort to raise levels of relevant trust. It will be recalled that clients often viewed God unhealthily or saw themselves as unacceptable to God. In other words, their deepest needs could be stated in terms of core belief. Whatever other systems of description a therapist may use, the terms and methods proposed and illustrated here have undeniably enriching possibilities.

Of course, the traditional suspicion with which therapists have held all religion was not and is not without some basis in fact. The cases reported on the preceding pages display the results of unhealthy religious teachings. However, the time has long since arrived for healers to make clear and responsible distinctions between good and bad belief systems—between traditional affirmations that are downright essential to wholeness, and others that hurt and harm. It should be fully understood that the latter are not and never have been valid interpretations of the biblically based Christian faith. These healing affirmations were not recently developed; they have been part of the Christian creed all along. To fail to include them in treating persons of faith is to overlook what could be the most potent resource possible.

This in turn suggests a radical challenge: that therapists carefully study and learn to use the best of the Christian belief system, since it is so deeply imbedded in the culture. Certainly the alternative to this leaves many in a religious vacuum, which bodes even greater evil than the presenting problem. Some will no doubt fear that this would seem dangerously nonobjective and unprofessional, but nothing could be further from the truth. The religious teaching or treatment proposed is subject to the most rigorous kinds of professional scrutiny, and what is taught would have only the most healing of impacts. To maintain clear professional standards, we must develop many mutually enriching and empowering exchanges between therapists and the teachers and practitioners of organized religion.

A final objection might be the therapist's understandable reluctance to resort to the tactics of media preachers. Therapists might rightly view both the preachers' techniques and their manipulative goals with repugnance. But there are other and more sensitive ways to communicate deep truth, and there are better versions of the eternal truth. Healing is not possible without some commitment to healthy core values.

Leaving the forceful, dramatic, public proclamation of the gospel to the divinely called and professionally trained ministers, there is still room for a quiet, vivid telling of such healing tales as that of Joseph in Genesis 50. In fact, just such an experience by a psychiatrist inspired this book's format. The therapist involved was no long-faced pietist or undeclared preacher. Earthy to the core, he yet saw nothing incongruous in telling a massively depressed patient that she evidenced visible signs of the love of her Creator. It was the only antidote he had for her belief that nobody loved her and that suicide seemed her best alternative, and it meshed with her traditional South European religious upbringing. The therapist was not preaching, but the patient knew he was very serious. It was the turning point to health for her.

Belief systems or theological formulations have much to offer the whole field of therapy. But therapists also have much to offer to theologians and to all facets of organized religion, as the following section shows.

Concerning Theology

Traditional theology has always leaned heavily first on divine revelation and then on reason. Whole systems have been built on basic posits from Scripture which then have been elaborated by reason or logic, presumably under the guidance of the Holy Spirit. Every traditional Christian position, from extreme right to extreme left, claims such a basis to a certain extent. This large spectrum reveals the wide variety of personal agenda and hidden assumptions that people bring to the theological task or the study of revelation. It also illustrates that many options are available inside the category called reason and suggests that substantial errors are possible within its processes.

To offset this potential for error, two correctives offer great hope: (1) Modern biblical scholarship emphasizes that Scripture as a whole and in context must be consulted before any passage can be adequately interpreted. The biblical context in every case includes all other passages related to this subject and their historical, cultural, and geographical contexts. (2) Interpretations of Scripture can be evaluated for their effects on human wholeness and spiritual health. It is at this particular point that this study would seem to have sweeping implications for theology. Even mentioning human welfare as a criterion for theological or doctrinal correction will cause some to object that this approach is humanist. For them, truth stands as abstract revelation outside human experience and human evaluation. To claim otherwise, they say, places people over God. The only adequate response to this valid concern points directly to Scripture. Jesus himself faced this issue in a confrontation with the Pharisees early in his ministry. The disciples had been picking and eating ears of corn on the Sabbath. The law of Jewish religion prohibited labor on this day, since it was set aside for the Lord and was to be observed by resting. Jesus responded with a clear indication that the rest was for the people of God, as was the day itself: "The Sabbath was made for man, and not man for the Sabbath" (Mark 2:23–28). God receives no glory from human undernourishment born of blind adherence to a law.

Jesus' words suggest that no theological statement is significant as abstract truth unrelated to the human struggle. God needs neither praise nor doctrine; they are both for human benefit. If a tenet of faith has no behavioral implications, it is not worth the trouble it takes to write it down. Every case cited in this work illustrates the relevance of doctrines for life. If God is provident, then people can live free of anxiety about survival and creaturely need. They can accept the struggles required in wholeness and joy. If God is just, then people can forget vengeance and remain faithful to the Christian principles of love no matter how much evil seems to flourish. Life always has meaning since "We shall reap" in due season, if we don't give up (Gal. 6:9). If God is omniscient, people can depend on being ultimately understood, even if no one on earth understands their real intent. Every doctrine that has emerged in the living world view is equally relevant to life.

Not unlike traditional theology, the most important attribute of God in Soul theology is grace. If people accept God's grace, they are made acceptable and given dignity and worth. There are no works or other conditions (Eph. 2:8). A media pastor from deep within the Calvinistic tradition, Robert H. Schuller, has aptly suggested the need for challenging the epidemic of alienation and self-hatred in his book *Self Esteem: The New Reformation*. Suggesting self-esteem as a midflight correction of the original Protestant Reformation, he defines it as the "human hunger for the divine dignity that God intended to be our emotional birthright as children in his image." (1982, 15, 25–26). Healthy self-esteem is made possible only by grace.

Turning to practical implications, Schuller insists that all theologies (of mission, of evangelism, of social ethics) depend on a central core of empowering self-acceptance (150). Jesus said the same thing when speaking of loving one's neighbor as oneself (Matt. 22:29). This idea is both clinically and biblically sound. It was long ignored, however, because of the traditional emphasis on human depravity growing out of an unbalanced theology. The result is that only thirty-five percent of Protestants show evidence that the church contributes to their self-esteem (Schuller 1982, 18), this "deepest of all human needs" (34). True spiritual revival and "reformation" must start with self-esteem.

The corrective proposed here emphasizes God's grace rather than human sinfulness on the ground that Jesus aimed prophetic criticism only at those who were overly proud and needed to be humbled. Someone has said that Jesus "comforted the afflicted and afflicted the comfortable." To a known transgressor already in the process of being crushed, he said, "Neither do I condemn thee" (John 8:11). His accepting response empowered her to live a better life, while a recital of the sins of which she was already painfully aware would have paralyzed her. The bottom line for theology and all of the rest of religion is that "nonjudgmental, unconditional love [grace] is the most healing force in the world" (Schuller 1982, 22). Every Bible doctrine or theological formulation must have that healing impact on the people for whom the Word was given in the first place, and no amount of linguistic or rational support can validate it otherwise.

Concerning Ministry

In addition to having therapeutic and theological benefits, new understandings of major affirmations of faith can strengthen programs of ministry as well as preachment. Our concern here is how to help people equip themselves with adequate, biblically based core belief systems so that they can become and remain emotionally and spiritually whole.

The most obvious starting place is Christian education. Denominational curricula can be used to plant the seeds of vital affirmations. Grading by age will be needed, of course. The process could begin with the goodness of God and nature among small children, moving on to the justice or fairness of God, and finally to the natural understanding and celebration of the more complicated themes of the Providence and grace of God. This may seem only slightly different from prevailing practice. The curriculum suggested here, however, is unabashedly committed to both deep core belief and the ability to discuss as well as feel a given affirmation. This is a very purposeful enterprise, with goals of a living, working faith that are not yet common in mainline Christian education programs.

Further, the curriculum suggested here would pay special attention to teaching methods. Children learn through their experience, more than through what they are told, and the teachers' attitudes of trust or core belief are more important to the working curriculum than the printed materials. Core belief is spread by contagion, and personal example can do what memory drills could never accomplish.

A twelve-year-old thus learned of the justice of God at a church-sponsored camp. His image of camping focused on playing pranks, and he had enjoyed his fill at first, including placing pepper on his father's pillow in the middle of the night. It all came to a screeching halt, however, when this boy was selected to be the object of one of the pranks. When the fun took place at his expense, he was utterly shattered. He tearfully reported to his leader and father, and he received a response that will never die in the minds of any of those campers: "Be not deceived; God is not mocked; for whatsoever a man soweth, that shall he also reap" (Gal. 6:7).

Given a good grasp of the crucial affirmations of Christian faith, coaches, advisors, choir directors, teachers, and ministers all have numberless opportunities to plant healing seed. The power of such experiences to shape life and trust is awesome. The potential for this kind of planting is limited largely by the leaders' level of personal core belief.

After Christian education, the next most obvious setting for planting healing affirmations in core belief is pastoral counseling. This role is greatly enhanced, of course, if the pastor and counselee can draw on accumulations of belief already planted through years of preaching and teaching. But even if no such history exists, the affirmations presented here are learned better late than never. In fact, the cry of the troubled father who brought his son to Jesus is the implicit request of almost every counselee: "Lord, I believe, help thou mine unbelief" (Mark 9:24). The world is full of people whose faith functions more in their minds than at the level of core belief, and often their cry expresses the split-level character of their working faith.

A lifelong Christian was wasting away, with no hope of a medical remedy. Although tests finally proved that he did not have cancer, the fears released by this possibility had stopped him from successfully eating or sleeping for three months. His already slim body was now dangerously depleted, and he was on his way to death. The church's counselor felt led to take the initiative, and he called to offer help. The sick man eagerly accepted, and with his remaining strength he drove immediately to the church office. He gladly poured out his case history, and together they discovered a sincerely felt guilt over a situation that was too small to have caused any disturbance whatever. But buried for years in the unconscious, it became punishable by death, to be carried out in self-imposed starvation, since the cancer had not materialized. The patient's problem was real and it required a serious cure directed to the core. No quick and easy mouthing of platitudes would do.

As with all guilt neuroses, the cure was the assurance of the grace of God, this time in the form of 1 John 1:9: "If we confess our sins, he is faithful and just to forgive us our sins, and to cleanse us from all unrighteousness." He was advised to read it often, and he soon memorized it in glad hunger. He was also advised to do the yard work so badly needed, no matter how weak he felt. He needed to be tired so he would have to sleep, and to be hungry so he would have to eat. The exertion broke the grip of the depression. The impact of this simple regimen exceeded everybody's fondest expectations. The man whom the physicians and psychiatrists could not help was back on the job in a little more than three weeks. Belief systems do have major influence on health, and pastoral counseling does not have to be unintelligently pietistic to take working cognizance of the fact.

Pastoral counseling will never replace professional therapy. But millions more can and should be helped than are presently being healed by either or both. The world is full of spiritually and emotionally wounded people whose core beliefs are in desperate need of strengthening and focus. This is a task that must be shared by sensitive and enlightened pastoral and other church-related counselors.

Concerning the Ministry of Worship

Churches have still another healing ministry of tremendous potential; it is called worship. Because worship is seldom recognized as a healing ministry, it frequently accomplishes this task in spite of rather than because of conscious intent. In many Soul churches, prayers and music are overly subordinated to preaching, to the extent of not being properly seen for what they can do to reinforce the affirmations of faith. In a word, worship is too often thought of as the warm-up, not the real game. Few church leaders are sensitive to the power of every worship service to mediate profound healing.

The prayers of the laity are much more significant than often recognized (cf. Carter 1976), and selected music has already been seen to be quite useful in affirmation therapy. Indeed, the prisoner and the entertainer quoted at the very outset of Chapter 1 were only living by the Bible affirmation (1 Cor. 10:13) paraphrased in the lyrics of the gospel song, "He Knows How Much You Can Bear." This suggests that a single song can be responsible for providing expression of, if not outright teaching, the trust of millions in the Providence and omniscience of God. The song's popularity is due in part to the music's way of replaying in the mind, but its greatest appeal is the way it helps people deal with the realities of a hard life.

Several of the cases cited included prescribed listening to taped songs of affirmation, since repeated listening is one of the best known ways of strengthening deep trust levels. Some hymns, of course, do not have this capability. But millions of people need so little help from healing professionals precisely because they are blessed with the habit of singing and humming their own therapeutic affirmations. When the old saints of Black churches wax ecstatic and shout over certain hymns, it is often because they sense the support this music has given them and are happy again at the very thought. Thus, if churches will carefully focus choices of music, prayer, and Scripture, the result could be the generating of healing beyond their fondest expectations.

Western worship has been dominated by the concern to offer "appropriate" ritual, poetry, and art for the praise of God. Soul tradition suggests that worship is most appropriate when it is most healing, since praise itself is remembrance and celebration of the goodness of life under God.

Concerning Ministry and the Family Model

In the context of church-related healing by training, counseling, and worship, it is only logical that many cases reported here were referred for follow-up to congregations known for caring in the manner of an extended family. Since unconditional love is the most healing force in the world, loving and caring congregation-families have healing power of awesome magnitude. This places on churches an equally awesome responsibility. If the ideal transition from regularly scheduled therapy to self-managed recovery is the family-church, then all too few churches are living up to that responsibility. Congregations more often minister to alcoholics or legal offenders when they have a mind for service. It is time for Christian churches to live up to their standing as the greatest hope society has for reaching and healing large numbers of ordinary troubled persons with unconditional love and enlightened care.

The ideal network for treatment is, of course, the home and family. The problem is that homes and families are usually directly responsible for illnesses in the first place. This clearly implies that churches must reach those homes with a kind of preventive ministry, rather than just to minister to the already disturbed youth or adult. To state it positively, the average person who enjoys wholeness has had the normal healing and preventive maintenance of a home with a parent or parents who were spiritually and emotionally whole. Churches must accept the challenge to enlarge the numbers of those homes in their memberships and communities.

Despite the tremendous power of love, a healing ministry is not easy. Healing love is not within the gift of many parents in churches, because they are not whole themselves and often are not ready to begin the disciplines necessary to become whole. Those who actually are ready and open will often find that they cannot grow fast enough to become what their children desperately need. The best hope for all concerned, then, is to plan concentrated effort in prayer and growth groups, drawing freely on the expertise of outside agencies. The congregation's goal should be no less than breaking the grip of the vicious cycle of the shortage of love, a problem that repeats itself generation after generation.

Along with the churches' help and agency resources, efforts within each nuclear family are crucial. Families cannot be remade from the outside. This will require some form of disci-

pline not entirely unlike the family devotions of several generations ago. Churches may have to teach family members how to
hear each other and together seek God's help for their growth.
Planned encounters with Bible verses may well have to come
back also. However, the dullness and routine that killed such
practices in the first place must be carefully avoided. We do not
need to repeat the mistakes of previous generations, where
children in families requiring a verse from each member before
the meal could start raced one another to see who could first
quote, "Jesus wept," the shortest verse in the Bible. Nor does
anyone need the sore knees some children had from kneeling
for marathon adult prayers. Many hungry children learned to
resent devotions because they were compulsory, and those
children are the parents and grandparents of today. Churches
will have to help them relearn shared spiritual disciplines of
greater interest, focus, and progressive maturing.

Perhaps the most important family change should be in the
casual conversations of everyday life. Affirmations shared in a
crisis or on a walk through the park may have more lasting
effect than the verses at table or in a class. When parents can
learn to break inhibitions about discussing trust and values,
they can use any time of the day to teach meaningfully as well
as to express their deep love. Indeed, the very survival of the
heritage of the Jewish faith as a world religion, across the centuries and the cultures, may be attributed to such a natural,
family-oriented process:

> And these words which I command thee this day, shall be in thine
> heart:
> And thou shalt teach them diligently unto thy children,
> And shalt talk of them when thou sittest in thine house,
> And when thou walkest by the way,
> And when thou liest down, and when thou risest up (Deut. 6:6–7).

Hank, twenty-six-year old-son of the senior author, was bat-
tling massive depression as he faced an already apparently losing struggle with leukemia. Alongside such major concerns as

the awful side effects of chemotherapy was his equally deep concern for the pain and sorrow of his parents. All efforts at concealing were to no avail, so he tried, as best he could, to turn the tables and minister to our need.

His favorite scheme was to interpret the situation in much the same way he had learned from his parents in childhood. He found an outlet for his parental concern and no little mischievous fulfillment for himself in giving exact quotations with penetrating relevance. "Didn't you guys used to tell me, God works in everything for good?" Then he would smile in mock triumph as he tried to keep all three of us from tears, and he would say, "Surely we aren't going to give up on that now, are we?" The fact is that he never did.

Hank had fully internalized the affirmation of God's Providence. He had attended church school faithfully, but he had probably not learned it there. No, nothing could match the impact of a belief uttered often in ordinary daily life by parents and grandparents. Time after time, resources had arrived just in time to provide for the children's activities. They did not have spare change jingling in their pockets, but they knew the large gifts always appeared at our poor parsonage right on time. The sources were unpredictable, but the resources arrived always without error.

Of course, we as parents missed very few opportunities to affirm the Providence just experienced, and we tried to do it always in a context of celebration, even fun. In fact, soon we did not have to say the speech at all. We would just laugh, and eventually some impatient child would do the honors of interpreting that experience by means of the Bible verse. Never really solemn, but always joyously serious, these occasions left indelible prints on the psyches and souls of four young preacher's kids. One of them showed the strength gained through it all as he walked trusting and unflinching to an early grave.

This story suggests the whole spectrum of implications for how therapy, theology, ministry, and families can prepare persons to deal with life's greatest stresses. The telling evidence of all that can be attempted by therapists and theologians, denominations and congregations, is best seen in how people respond to stress—how well their core beliefs support them and provide loving, family-style support networks. The only alternative for those with no blood kin will be a church willing to welcome them into the loving, caring extended family that every congregation should be striving to become. Where else can a person learn and keep the faith, rooted and grounded in the affirmations that empower abundant living?

In Summary

For all too long, too many religious leaders of the Western world have assumed that spiritual wholeness and emotional balance could be achieved by rational argument. No matter what lip service may have been paid to other means, this was the basic approach. Yet the persons who have borne stress most nobly in our society have been nurtured and equipped for life by a kit of affirmations taught spontaneously in a stream of culture. It is true, of course, that if the teaching had been incoherent it would not have survived. So reason was not abandoned here. However, the primary appeal of these affirmations of faith lay not in their coherence but in their ability to sustain life and make it worth living.

The studies and cases shared here have, we hope, established the importance of holistically addressing and healing people in the depths of core belief. Public worship and private family life and all resources of time and concern must be focused on recapturing a culturewide positive world view. We must recover the faith that has for centuries sustained and healed members of the Soul culture, and this healing approach must be shared with all humanity. Selah.

SELECT BIBLIOGRAPHY

Carter, Harold A. *The Prayer Tradition of Black People*. Valley Forge, Pennsylvania: Judson Press, 1976.

Cone, James H. *The Spirituals and the Blues*. New York: Seabury Press, 1972.

Gendlin, Eugene T. *Focusing*. New York: Bantam Books, 1981.

Haley, Alex. *Roots*. Garden City, NY: Doubleday & Co., Inc., 1976.

Harris, Joel Chandler. *Uncle Remus*. New York: Meredith Press, 1880, 1921.

Iacocca, Lee. *Iacocca*. New York: Bantam Books, 1984.

Liebow, Elliot. *Tally's Corner*. Boston: Little, Brown & Co., 1967.

Little, Sara. *To Set One's Heart*. Atlanta: John Knox Press, 1983.

Lucas, Bob. "Lola Falana Talks about Life without a Man." *Jet Magazine* 57 No. 1 (20 September 1979):25. Cf. also Vol. 57, No. 13 (December 13, 1979):53, and Vol. 64, No. 19 (July 18, 1983):61.

Mitchell, Henry H. *Black Belief*. New York: Harper & Row, 1975.

Mowrer, O. Hobart. *The Crisis in Psychiatry and Religion*. Princeton: D. Van Nostrand Co., Inc., 1961.

Pattison, E. Mansell and Myrna L. Pattison. "Analysis of a Schizophrenic Psychosocial Network." *Schizophrenia Bulletin* 7, No. 1 (1981):135–43.

St. Cyr, Sylvester. *The Saint and Sinners*. New York: Vantage Press, 1972.

Schuller, Robert H. *Self Esteem: The New Reformation*. Waco, Texas: Word Books, 1982.

Subject Index

Scripture Index

Index to Spirituals

Index to Hymns and Gospel Songs